SPIRITUALISM &
CLAIRVOYANCE
for Beginners

About the Author

Elizabeth Owens is a certified medium and an ordained Spiritualist minister. She teaches spiritual development classes in the Cassadaga Spiritualist Camp in Cassadaga, Florida, where she also resides.

SPIRITUALISM & CLAIRVOYANCE
for Beginners

Simple Techniques to Develop Your Psychic Abilities

Elizabeth Owens

Llewellyn Publications
St. Paul, Minnesota

First Edition
First Printing, 2005

Book design and layout by Joanna Willis
Cover design by Ellen Dahl
Cover images © 2005 by Comstock Images and DigitalStock

Llewellyn is a registered trademark of Llewellyn Worldwide, Ltd.

Library of Congress Cataloging-in-Publication Data
Owens, Elizabeth, 1948–
  Spiritualism & clairvoyance for beginners: simple techniques to
  develop your psychic abilities.—1st ed.
     p. cm.
  Includes bibliographical references.
  ISBN 0-7387-0707-4
  1. Psychic ability. 2. Spiritualism. 3. Clairvoyance.
  I. Title: Spiritualism and clairvoyance for beginners. II. Title.
  BF1031.094 2005
  133.8—dc22   2005043584

Llewellyn Worldwide does not participate in, endorse, or have any authority or responsibility concerning private business transactions between our authors and the public.
  All mail addressed to the author is forwarded but the publisher cannot, unless specifically instructed by the author, give out an address or phone number.
  Any Internet references contained in this work are current at publication time, but the publisher cannot guarantee that a specific location will continue to be maintained. Please refer to the publisher's website for links to authors' websites and other sources.

Llewellyn Publications
A Division of Llewellyn Worldwide, Ltd.
P.O. Box 64383, Dept. 0-7387-0707-4
St. Paul, MN 55164-0383, U.S.A.
www.llewellyn.com

Printed in the United States of America

Other Books in the For Beginners Series

Astrology for Beginners
William W. Hewitt

Chakras for Beginners
David Pond

Divination for Beginners
Scott Cunningham

Healing Alternatives for Beginners
Kay Henrion

Magick for Beginners
J. H. Brennan

Meditation for Beginners
Stephanie Clement

Practical Magic for Beginners
Brandy Williams

Psychic Development for Beginners
William W. Hewitt

Contents

Preface

Clairvoyance is a natural gift for some people and a talent that may be cultivated by those who have the desire. In simple terms, *clairvoyance* is a French word meaning "clear seeing." It is the art of seeing spirit entities, which may or may not be visible through the eyes of others. Clairvoyance also includes the ability to see, in our mind's eye, colors, symbols, numbers, words, faces, and scenes.

This ability has been around since the beginning of time but came into prominence in the United States when the Fox sisters shot to fame after receiving communication from a murdered peddler who was buried in the basement of their home. The religion of Spiritualism grew from that communication and has since caused millions to consider the possibility of life after death and the benefits of communicating with those who are behind the veil. Clairvoyance is one method in which we may receive communication from our loved ones who are in the spirit world.

Many people experience spontaneous clairvoyance as children. The lucky few who did not lose the ability upon reaching adulthood continue to experience clairvoyance. By no means is this some bizarre occurrence that identifies such people as weird. If you are an adult who experiences spontaneous clairvoyance, please understand that you are not abnormal. Quite the contrary, you are gifted.

There is nothing to be afraid of concerning the development of clairvoyance. Fear is ignorance. We fear what we cannot understand. *Spiritualism & Clairvoyance* will clear away the confusion and help answer your questions. You will find that developing clairvoyance or enhancing the ability you already possess has many practical advantages. There are so many ways that clairvoyance can be utilized in our daily lives to make our existences easier. Did you know that we can call upon our clairvoyant abilities to determine the cause of a problem in our car?

Whether you have a desire to enhance a natural clairvoyant ability or to develop the gift of clairvoyance, exercises are offered to aid in that quest. There is a workbook format at the end of most of the chapters where experiences can be recorded after completion of the exercises. The last chapter is dedicated entirely to offering exercises for practice.

The very first time one attempts an exercise, it is not uncommon to "see," but hold on . . . that doesn't make you a professional clairvoyant! I only mention this possibility to emphasize that clairvoyance is a natural ability. You further develop this useful talent through practice and dedication.

Life is a journey, and by completing the exercises in this book, it is my hope that you will create a better existence for yourself. We already have the power to make changes in our lives. All we have to do is learn to focus that energy!

I extend warm blessings to you for a better, better, and better life!

Acknowledgments

With the warmest of gratitude, I recognize the mediums from the Cassadaga Spiritualist Camp who participated in this book. Their input was so valuable to its creation. My heartfelt thanks to the following people: Rev. Phoebe Rose Bergin; Rev. Diane Davis; Rev. Dr. Warren Hoover; Rev. Arlene Sikora; and Rev. Jim Watson.

A special thank you goes to my dear friend in Milwaukee, Wisconsin, who is a well-known medium in that area—Carol Roberts, thank you so very much for sharing!

It has been a pleasure to receive e-mails and letters from the readers of my books. Thank you so much for sharing your delight and experiences with me.

Many thanks to Llewellyn Worldwide for continuing to publish my books and for the fabulous cover designs.

As always, thank you, Vincent, my best friend and husband.

Namaste.

one

How It All Began

Clairvoyance is a natural ability. It has been with us since humans first walked the earth, but I can't imagine that prehistoric people were consciously aware of this form of communication. In my mind, prehistoric men and women were souls on a trial run. This was an experiment for souls to occupy a physical body so they could learn lessons on another plane of existence. Since development is achieved more quickly here on earth than it is in the spirit world, earth would have provided the perfect place to take a physical form and learn.

As the earth evolved, so did our species. Eventually, human beings became aware of some of their more unique abilities—abilities that set them apart from the animal and plant kingdoms. Besides intelligence, they came to realize that one ability they possessed was intuition. Perhaps they talked about their abilities, and maybe they didn't. If they did talk, maybe one of the abilities they mentioned was being able to "see" things that were not readily visible to the human eye. This would make one wonder whether or not the others in the conversation also saw things. If they shared this experience of seeing, then a dialog began. If no one shared this experience, the one person who was seeing was probably chastised or ridiculed, maybe even ostracized. But, again, this is merely speculation on my part about the possibilities in those ancient times.

There are numerous examples in the Bible of spiritual visitations and prophetic declarations. It is also true that Nostradamus and other enlightened people of their day predicted events. But in 1848 a phenomenon occurred that indirectly introduced the United States to clairvoyance and all things that are psychic, and we haven't been the same since. The phenomenon was called "spirit raps," and these raps emanated from within the home of the Fox family. The interest that grew from the phenomenon was so intense, and the need for people to be reassured that there was indeed an afterlife was so profound, that it created a religion with millions of devoted followers and even changed many people's thinking about the hereafter.

The phenomenon began while Mr. and Mrs. John D. Fox and their two young daughters were temporarily residing in a modest cottage in Hydesville, New York, while their new house was being built. Shortly after moving into the cottage, the family heard odd noises, movements, rappings, and felt vibrations. The longer they lived in the cottage, the more intense and persistent the racket became, thus making sleep impossible. The girls, Margaretta, fourteen, and Catherine (Katie), twelve, were growing tired of the disturbances, so they brought some levity to the situation on the night of March 31, 1848. Katie clapped her hands and demanded of what she thought to be a spirit, "Mr. Splitfoot, do as I do!"

Immediately the spirit imitated the raps. Margaretta joined in the fun now, also ordering the spirit to follow her lead. She began to count out loud as she clapped her hands. The raps responded in kind again.

Mrs. Fox began to participate, asking questions of the spirit and also receiving raps in response. She and her daughters devised a code, and eventually Mrs. Fox was able to determine that the spirit creating the raps was a peddler who had been murdered for his goods five years prior when he was thirty-two years of age. His name was Charles Rosna. He further relayed that his body could be found buried in the cellar.

News of this remarkable phenomenon traveled far and wide. Hundreds converged upon Hydesville, New York, to witness spirit communication by the Fox sisters. Word of these unusual happenings reached Leah Fox, an older daughter living in Rochester, New York. Leah traveled to Hydesville for the purpose of bringing some order into the family's peculiar situation. Leah's plan was to bring her mother and sister Katie back to Rochester with her. Margaretta was to remain behind with their brother, David, who lived in a house nearby. Leah hoped that by separating the sisters the disturbances would cease. But the spirits apparently had another plan. With only Katie present in Leah's home, the raps continued. At this point it seemed fruitless to continue to separate the sisters, so they were reunited in Rochester.

One evening the family decided to call out the letters of the alphabet in an attempt to receive a message from the spirit world. The spirits were obviously so eager to communicate, they persisted even in the new location. The message they received instructed them to inform the world of the truths the sisters were receiving, because this was a new era. For serving their duty, the spirits promised that God would protect the Fox sisters, plus good spirits would watch over them.

Katie and Margaretta found that their psychic abilities developed rapidly, and manifestations continually occurred. It was a very exciting time for all who were involved. Famous and influential people of the day were attracted to the Fox sisters, and a religion was subsequently formed: Spiritualism.

Isaac and Amy Post, the famous abolitionists, were among the well-known people of the time who became friends and ardent supporters of the Fox sisters. Amy Post was to become known in later years as the Mother of Modern Spiritualism.

The Fox girls were involved in the first public meeting of Spiritualists held on November 14, 1849, at Corinthian Hall, the largest hall in Rochester, New York. On June 4, 1850, Katie and Margaretta brought their demonstrations and Spiritualism to New York, where many celebrities gathered to experience a séance. Horace Greeley, the editor of the *New York Tribune*, was the first to participate. Consequently, he became an avid follower and was instrumental in publicizing the message of Spiritualism to the residents of New York and other states. Many other mediums also sprang to the forefront, eventually introducing mediumship and the message of Spiritualism to millions.

When Spiritualism first began, it became apparent that a phenomenon was rampant. It is claimed that at that time the spirit world felt it was necessary to give people proof that they did not die, but merely went on to another life-form, so the spirits performed remarkable feats to convince people that they, the spirits, were still alive. A message from someone's mother that only the recipient could understand, instructions on where to find a missing locket, lost will and testament, or other valuable documents and items are examples of the types of messages that were received. Whatever it took to get people's attention, the spirits did it. Objects floated in séance rooms, tables bounced on one leg, spirits manifested and spoke aloud. All this happened through the abilities of a medium.

In bygone years, it was common for those who sought solace over the death of a child, husband, or relative to seek out the services of a medium who could bridge the two worlds together. The knowledge that a loved one was content, not in pain, and growing brought great comfort to the bereaved seekers. Any messages that were received were welcomed beyond ecstasy. To learn that a husband still loved and cared for his wife and even looked after her from the other world was a message that brought immeasurable comfort.

Mediumship had many facets in those days, and still does today, in which an individual may demonstrate his or her talents. One of those talents was, and is, clairvoyance. This book is dedicated to informing you, the reader, about clairvoyance and assisting you in the development of this wonderful gift. Whether you are currently aware that you have natural clairvoyant abilities or desire to develop the talent of clairvoyance, this book will help you in either of these endeavors. Clairvoyance assists us in the development of keener awareness; there is less confusion and more accuracy in the decisions we make. Many common daily problems can be solved through clairvoyance. By developing clairvoyance, we have an opportunity for a peaceful existence instead of yo-yoing around, plus we are healthier, happier, and have more creative potential. The sky's the limit!

Rev. Jim Watson, a Spiritualist minister, feels that we can gain significant insight through clairvoyance. By utilizing the talent of clairvoyance, we can gain awareness so we are better prepared for what is coming. In this manner we are guiding our own lives, being co-creators in our own existence. Jim says that the biblical phrase "Ask and you shall receive" is a perfect example in reference to clairvoyance. Whatever our intention is, ask for that guidance or answer, and the vision will be laid out in front of us. Once we learn to interpret what we are given in meditation, we don't have to search out answers because they are shown to us. Clairvoyance makes life easier by making this a part of our reality.

Throughout the book I will include comments from six mediums, and I will also comment. Five of the mediums reside and work in the historic community called the Southern Cassadaga Spiritualist Camp, in Cassadaga, Florida. It is the oldest and only active religious community in the south. Its warm history dates back to 1894. The five mediums you will hear from are the Rev. Arlene Sikora, the Rev. Dr. Warren Hoover, the Rev. Diane Davis, the Rev. Phoebe Rose Bergin, and the Rev. Jim Watson. The sixth medium lives in Milwaukee, Wisconsin, and her name is Carol Roberts, a very dear friend of mine and a fabulous medium. In order for you to become acquainted with these people, I will relay the circumstances of when each of them first became aware of his or her clairvoyant abilities.

Phoebe first saw spirits during her early childhood years. There was one particular Native American that she remembers standing very tall in the corner of her bedroom. She asked her mother about this Indian standing in the corner, and her mother said it was nothing to be afraid of, that it was a spirit guide that would protect her. She even told Phoebe the name of the guide, which was Red Wing. Phoebe's mother also reassured her by saying that spirits would continue in her life and she would see them off and on. Knowing that the spirits were there to take care of her was comforting to Phoebe.

Phoebe definitely grew up in an unusually open family with beliefs and practices that the average child would never have been exposed to. The reason Phoebe experienced such unusual exposure was because her mother was a medium. It all began when Phoebe's parents were seeking their truth, so they investigated other religions when they were living in New York. They met a well-known Spiritualist medium, Clifford Bias, while attending his home circle on 44th Street in New York City. Phoebe's mother also traveled to Lily Dale, in New York, and Camp Silver Bell, in Ephrata, Pennsylvania, which were established Spiritualist Camps at that time, in her search for more information and developmental experiences.

Phoebe's father, at the opposite end of the spectrum, was more of a skeptic. He didn't want "wispy curtain things," Phoebe said; he demanded substantial proof. However, he became a believer on the night the couple attended a particular séance where four different objects floated up and around the room. One of those objects was a victrola. Then he believed!

Phoebe was six or seven years old when her family moved to the city to live in a small apartment. It was in this apartment that Phoebe remembers her mother holding small séances. Phoebe heard and watched as her mother's voice changed when an Indian guide and other teacher guides channeled through her mother. Such was the exposure for Phoebe as a child, probably quite different from your own!

During her childhood, the Rev. Arlene Sikora also saw spirits, as I mentioned in my book *How to Communicate with Spirits*. When she was six years old, her grandmother passed into the spirit world. At the wake, Arlene saw her grandmother standing on the staircase. She wondered why everyone was so upset and crying if her grandmother was right there. She mentioned to someone that her grandmother was standing on the staircase, but received no response.

After the wake, Arlene began to receive almost nightly visits from her grandmother for nearly a year. Her grandma would routinely stand at the foot of her bed, which naturally scared Arlene. When she told her parents about these visitations, they could not offer an explanation. Eventually, Arlene denied her reality and the visitations ceased until she was eleven, which is when they moved to Florida. In Florida, the visits began again, only this time she appeared in a cloud hovering above Arlene. Usually she would extend her hand down to Arlene and call to her. Well, understandably, this really terrified Arlene! She went to her parents again, but did not receive any answers that satisfied her. To save her sanity, Arlene once again denied her reality and the visits ceased. It wasn't until Arlene became an adult that she began seeking answers to the experiences she encountered as a young child.

When the Rev. Jim Watson was a little boy, he saw spirits out of the corner of his eyes. Being around six years of age, he did not have enough knowledge to actually understand what he was seeing. Whenever he saw a spirit and pointed it out to someone, the other person would say that nobody was there. Jim doesn't remember ever being chastised by his parents for revealing his experiences, and it was never suggested that these occurrences were something you weren't supposed to talk about, either.

Despite the lack of confirmation from adults, it seemed natural to Jim that spirits were around, and he continued to see spirits. Once he saw a couple standing outside who he thought lived in a house across the street. Jim was promptly told that the two had been dead for years.

At the age of six, Jim saw his great-great-grandmother in spirit. He described the experience as being similar to seeing a shadow image. It was similar to a negative of a photograph, sort of transparent. It definitely did not look like a flesh and blood person. Jim talked to his great-grandmother, who was living in his family's home, about what he had seen and what the spirit was wearing. The great-grandmother accepted this information, acknowledging that Jim's great-great-grandmother would have worn those clothes. She also stated, casually, that she was aware that Jim's great-great-grandmother came around at times.

At this young age, Jim's innocence allowed him to accept that these occurrences were natural happenings. Jim continued to experience episodes throughout his life as he matured, and even then he didn't give it much attention because he still thought it was natural. One thing that no doubt helped Jim believe in the naturalness of seeing spirits was that he had a friend who also saw spirits, and they would talk about what they saw. It's not surprising that when Jim reached his twenties, he started reading about ghosts, hauntings, and phenomena. In his mid-thirties, Jim went to the church in Cassadaga and was exposed to a whole religion built around communication with spirits. It was there that he sought to further develop his abilities.

The Rev. Diane Davis was a natural intuitive as a child. She remembers experiencing a knowingness about certain things when she was about six years old. This knowingness was very pronounced and was usually followed by a synchronistic event. Once, when she was visiting the Heard

Museum in Phoenix, Arizona, the museum was conduct-
ing a cakewalk for the children, so Diane entered the cakewalk contest. When she looked over toward the array of
cakes lined up for the winners, she saw a chocolate cake.
Immediately, Diane knew that she would win that particular cake, and she did.

It wasn't until some years later, when Diane was an adult,
that she began taking meditation classes in Cassadaga. At
first she started classes for the purpose of self-growth and
personal improvement. She did not have a preconceived
idea of what would happen, nor did she have any expectations. However, things certainly did happen! She was so accurate the first time in class that she was classified as a natural intuitive. Within six months of attending classes, Diane
was discerning spirits.

One thing that has always impressed me about Diane is
that she is always so "on." She is a true sensitive in the best
definition of that term. She senses as we talk or as she
goes about her day. When obstacles impede her way in
life, she psychometrizes the situation, receives inspiration,
and is better able to deal with the problem. Her sensitivity
is acute, and it works for her highest and best endeavors
every day of her life.

The Rev. Dr. Warren Hoover also saw spirits objectively
and subjectively when he was a child; this started when he
was six years old. He experienced visions, too, although not
of any great world consequence. The visions he received

were usually family related and typically came through a dream. His first experience seeing a spirit was when his older brother died. The brother's spirit walked through the bedroom door, over to Warren's bed, and then spoke to him. Warren could actually hear the words he said. The purpose for this spirit visitation was so the brother could come back to tell Warren that he was okay. Even though Warren was only six, he said he knew what he saw and heard, and could not be persuaded otherwise. That's what ignited Warren's curiosity about the spirit world.

Warren was fortunate, like Phoebe, to have a medium for a mother. Warren's mother became involved with Spiritualism when she was eighteen, and spent time at Camp Silver Bell. Therefore, when Warren told her about the visitation from his brother, she was not the least bit upset, accepting it as fact.

Warren's natural abilities continued into adulthood, but he did not pursue any formal studies for further development until a neighbor talked about having gone to Camp Silver Bell. The neighbor described the phenomena he had witnessed at the camp. This really caught Warren's attention, and he began his formal development studies.

As a child, Carol Roberts experienced déjà vu. She would walk into a room she hadn't been in before and would know where every piece of furniture was located. This sort of experience would leave Carol feeling like she had been in the room before, except she hadn't. Carol frequently knew what was around the corner before she actually turned the corner. At the tender age of seven or eight, these experiences scared her. When Carol mentioned these occurrences to her father, he shared with her that it was okay to experience these sorts of things. He stated that the same things used to happen to him when he was a boy. Naturally, that made Carol feel better, and, consequently, she was able to accept her experiences as normal occurrences.

In Carol's young life, many things happened that proved she had natural abilities. Although Carol was the youngest sibling in the family, she felt more mature than her two older sisters and always felt like she knew more than they did. It was a puzzle to her why they didn't know certain things.

Carol had unusual premonitions. For instance, when she was in the eighth grade, she saw the boy who would become her husband in years to come. Carol only saw him from the back, yet she grabbed her girlfriend's arm and said, "That's the guy I'm going to marry." She simply knew certain things that were beyond her years of experience.

When Carol was in high school, friends would ask questions about their love lives, such as, "Will he call me again?" Carol would say, "Don't worry, he'll call," or "Sorry, but he won't be calling you." Somehow she always knew whether or not a guy would call. Afterward she would wonder how she knew this information but her girlfriends didn't. Carol always put these experiences aside so she wouldn't be too different from everyone else. It wasn't until some years later, after the difficult delivery of her son, that Carol began reading about and exploring the psychic realms.

When I was about twenty years old, I became fascinated with astrology. Although I never became proficient enough in the science of astrology to do charts, I learned a lot about people by studying their sun signs and ascendants. Later on, I received a reading from a wonderful medium when I lived in Orlando, Florida. I was so intrigued by the experience that I decided I wanted to do what she did. I wanted to be a medium. So, I began classes with her. During the classes I discovered that although I didn't remember seeing spirits as a child, the images I was seeing were familiar to me—they were the very same sensations I had when I was a child sitting alone in my bedroom. I also remember hearing "sounds" downstairs. What I experienced in meditation was familiar, yet new.

My parents were as far removed from Spiritualism as Warren's and Phoebe's parents were involved in it. I have no doubt that if I had mentioned one thing that I saw or felt from the spirit world, my parents would have told me that it was just my imagination. My proper mother would have been horrified, and would have banished those thoughts from my brain. This may be why I have no memories of seeing spirits at a young age, but I do remember the sensations.

two

Defining Clairvoyance

Clairvoyance is the art of seeing with senses beyond the five that we normally use, and is often referred to as the "sixth sense." Clairvoyance is a word derived from two French words, *clair* and *voyance*, giving us the definition of "clear seeing." *The Encyclopedia of Psychic Science*, by Nandor Fodor, states that clairvoyance is "a supernormal mode of perception, which results in a visual image being presented to the conscious mind. The perception may be of objects or forms distant in space, or in time, past or future."

Many say that when we see clairvoyantly we are using the third eye. The third eye is actually a gland known as the pineal gland, which is located in the back area of the brain, almost in the center of the head, and sits about an inch above our two eyes, hence the term "third eye." When this area begins to "open up" during the developmental stage, we sometimes experience an itch or tingle on the surface of the skin on our forehead.

Clairvoyance is associated with the right side of the brain, which holds our feminine, creative, and intuitive aspects. It is normal to feel physical sensations on the left side of the body when working clairvoyantly because energy enters in through the left side of the body, thus making the left side our receiver. This energy activates the right side of the brain. Clairvoyance identifies messages, shapes, colors, symbols, numbers, and objects from other realms. The images may remain visible for a while or only a few seconds, and are seen with the eyes open or closed.

Carol defines clairvoyance, as a whole, as the ability to step out of where we are and into other energy fields. She states that "we have to put who we are aside, our thoughts, cares, and troubles, in order to be a receptive vessel. We then feel and share the emotions of the person to whom we are giving a reading. There is no thought of our ego, only the great desire to heal."

Although a person may experience clairvoyance in many ways, there are two basic categories. Those two categories are objective clairvoyance and subjective clairvoyance.

Objective Clairvoyance

Objective clairvoyance is when a medium is capable of literally seeing spirit entities that are unseen by others with their physical eyes. This ability to literally see spirits is considered to be an uncommon gift. According to Spiritualist references, objective clairvoyance is when objects and spirits from the spiritual realm are seen through the spiritual senses, bypassing the physical mechanism of the eyes.

Warren defines objective clairvoyance as actually seeing with the physical eyes—the vibration follows the nerve centers to the eyes so that one can literally see the spirit entity. Arlene defines objective clairvoyance as the ability to see a spirit that is not normally visible to others, but it's there. She also feels that it is helpful to be "at onement" in order to perceive the spirit.

An example of objective clairvoyance would be Bettie's experience. During the middle of the night, Bettie was having difficulty sleeping, which was not unusual for her, so she got out of bed and began walking around the house in the dark. As she was returning down the hallway toward the bedroom, she almost walked into a spirit entity that was walking in the hallway at the same time. Bettie saw the spirit very plainly standing before her. She said hello. The spirit nodded, and then dissolved into the air. That is objective clairvoyance; Bettie literally *saw* a spirit.

Bettie is not a professional medium, nor was she attempting to communicate with any spirits. She just couldn't sleep and was walking around her house, oblivious to most everything she walked by. Bettie did not recognize the spirit she saw in the hallway, which is not uncommon. The spirit was probably "passing through" and Bettie just happened to be around at the time. However, Bettie has seen spirits all of her life. This is a natural gift for her, and one she doesn't desire to cultivate further.

Anyone could see a spirit. It could be a fleeting glimpse out of the corner of the eye, or a wisp of something quickly passing by, as Jim Watson experienced as a child (see chapter 1). It is not uncommon for spirits to jostle us to attention in this manner. When I was twenty-two, I lived in an apartment over a restaurant. One night I awoke and turned over in bed. In the doorway stood a young woman with blond hair, dressed in white. She didn't move, nor did she say anything, but it freaked me out all the same. I turned over and pulled my bedcovers up higher. I wanted her to go away. When I finally conjured up the nerve to turn over toward her, I saw that she was gone.

Although she had given me a fright, I was curious enough to do some investigating. I asked the owners of the restaurant for information about the young woman, but no one knew anything about her. There was an empty room above my apartment, so I walked up there to explore. I don't remember finding anything significant there, and I didn't run into the spirit again, either. Even though I am a professional medium, I have yet to literally see another spirit. Whoever that spirit was, she certainly got my attention, though, and I have written about her numerous times.

If you have experienced a similar circumstance where you saw or heard a spirit that could not be identified and wondered why it happened, it is a sign that you have some unexercised and undiscovered talents that need to be developed. It can also be a sign that there is more to this world than what we normally accept, and you are being enlightened. The following example fits this explanation to a tee.

When Phoebe married, she chose a man named Bill. He was Catholic, and a nonbeliever in the psychic—he thought it was all just a bunch of hocus pocus. One day Bill was curious enough, though, to ask Phoebe's mother if he had a spirit guide. She gave Bill the name of his Indian guide and his description. Nothing really came of that knowledge until a couple of years later, when Phoebe and Bill were living in Connecticut.

Bill's job required him to drive sixty to seventy thousand miles a year. One day while on the road, he heard a voice say, "Step on the gas and move over." He looked around to see where the voice was coming from. He didn't have the radio on and nobody was riding in the cab with him. Then Bill heard the command again, and this time it was much stronger. He decided to move over one lane. Just then a tire fell off of a truck that was driving on the other side of the highway. The tire rolled by him, narrowly missing his truck by inches.

Bill reportedly broke out in a sweat and said, "You know, I think there's something to this. I think that guide, that Indian, was with me."

Bill also had the opportunity to experience seeing his sister and mother—who were both in spirit—as he was walking to the bathroom just three days prior to his passing. When he told Phoebe, she was delighted that he had experienced that visit from his family, and that he was now a believer—but it was the truck tire that made the biggest impression on Bill!

It is common for our loved ones to gather around us when we are close to our passing. Many people have had the experience of observing a dying relative seemingly speaking into the air to someone who has passed away. Perhaps the person identifies several relatives who are in spirit, but only he or she sees the spirits.

Widows frequently have encounters with the spirits of their recently deceased husbands. It is common for the spirits of people we have known in the past to come calling on us to see how we are doing because the spirit that once resided in a physical body on the earthplane continues to love us when in spirit. The spirit wants to know how we are and what we are doing, so it may present itself so that we can literally see it. However, actually *seeing* a spirit is probably a one-time occasion. It is not necessarily an indication that we possess objective clairvoyance.

Since objective clairvoyance is not a common occurrence, I would equate it to having a beautiful singing voice. An opera singer's voice, for instance, is a true vocal gift—one that is essentially reserved for the select. During the late 1800s and up until the 1960s it was much more common than it is today to literally see spirits. However, the energy on the earth has shifted greatly, what we eat has changed, and the environment has many more pollutants—all of these factors contributed to the decline in incidents of objective clairvoyance.

Objective clairvoyance cannot be willfully developed any more than we can all sing like Celine Dion. After all, the spirit world does have some controls. If a spirit does not want to manifest in front of us, it won't. There is absolutely no way to compel a spirit to manifest. If that were possible, believe me, I know many people who would stand in line for that experience! It just isn't possible to teach someone to have objective clairvoyance. However, over time and with practice, it is possible that the spirit world will bless you with this gift.

A medium I know who has been in the practice for twelve years recently encountered a spirit while she was on her way to the bathroom in the middle of the night. (There must be something significant about walking around in the middle of the night!) She was quite surprised—but equally delighted—to actually see the spirit. This was a first for her, and, hopefully, a beginning.

Subjective Clairvoyance

The more common clairvoyant ability is subjective clairvoyance. According to Spiritualist references, the formal explanation of subjective clairvoyance is when spiritual entities manipulate the nerve centers of the eyes to impress upon the brain images that are not seen by the physical eyes. This is where a person "sees" pictures, images, numbers, words, colors, people, and so forth in his or her mind. This can be more of a fleeting impression. Subjective clairvoyance may occur with the eyes closed or open. This form of clairvoyance also may come spontaneously or can be induced through meditation. Since subjective clairvoyance is a far more common ability, it is one I believe everyone can develop, to a certain extent.

Sometimes when we watch a medium delivering messages to people in the audience during a message service, we hear the medium say, "I see your grandmother standing beside you." The medium isn't truly "seeing" the grandmother. In all probability, the medium is receiving a visual in his or her mind that the grandmother is standing next to the person. He or she is not literally seeing the spirit. To say, "I see _____ standing . . ." is a common phrase we use when demonstrating public message work.

Phoebe sees subjective colors, scenes, and people, although she rarely sees symbols. During a reading, Phoebe prefers to have her eyes closed so that she is not influenced by the reaction of the client. By working with her eyes closed, her concentration is totally on what she is seeing in her mind's eye.

Warren experiences both forms of clairvoyance, depending upon the vibrations and his awareness and alertness at the time. He defines subjective clairvoyance as sometimes more vague and ethereal, since we are seeing with the mind's eye. When I interviewed Warren, he mentioned that the pineal gland contains germanium crystals and responds to electrical vibrations. Germanium crystals are still used today in electronics. These crystals respond to vibrations or metal forms and are sensitive to electronic signals. In the body, they are sensitive enough to pick up a spirit entity or personality, or a psychic vibration. All this happens in the pineal gland.

Arlene is privileged to see objectively and subjectively also. Sometimes, she says, spirits appear in a solid form during readings, and other times they appear within the conscious mind. Spirits will pop up unexpectedly at odd times while Arlene is going about her day even outside of the reading room, but spontaneous appearances do not surprise Arlene because they happen so frequently.

From the age of two until about seven, sometimes even nine, it is natural for children to have mystical and spiritual experiences. This is because it hasn't been that long since they were on the spiritual side, so they are open to receive. The Rev. Diane Davis remembers that as a child she would talk all day long on a toy telephone to a "friend" whom no one else could see.

Arlene knows that small children, especially, see spirits easily. After all, she had that experience herself. The ability is strongest when children are six, seven, or eight. Of course, the ability has been there all along, but it really becomes identifiable around the age of seven.

Sometimes children are frightened by what they see, and they also frighten their parents when they relay their experiences. Many times the parents aren't familiar with or know people involved in this type of spiritual work. Some parents go to Carol Roberts for guidance and to gain an understanding of these matters. After they speak with Carol, they are relieved to know that other people have experienced these unique events. Consequently, the children are happy again once they know that they aren't weird or that their parents aren't going to punish them for claiming to see something their parents cannot.

If childhood clairvoyant experiences were recognized by society as a spiritual process and deemed as natural and the truth of human reality, then clairvoyance would be a common ability for everyone. If children were allowed to stay open and receptive, the natural ability to see spirits would not go away, such as was the case with Phoebe's and Warren's experiences during childhood. Unfortunately, some parents are not enlightened, and when a child insists that "Uncle Joe" is standing in the doorway, they merely tell the child that nothing is there. Eventually, children deny what they see and as adults often forget that they ever did see spirits.

All of us agreed that every child sees spirits until an adult tells the child that it's only his or her imagination. Some advice to parents is to never say, "You're just imagining this, hallucinating. There is no playmate there." Because we trust parental judgment and see our parents as all wise and knowing, we accept what our parents say and close the door to anything that conflicts with their version of the truth. Let us strive to observe our children's abilities and not discourage what they see in the spirit world. We all see and experience these things when we are very young, we just don't always remember.

Warren feels that the exposure children have today makes them more open and accepting of the spirit world. What with television, radio, and the movies, kids today are exposed to lots of psychic things. Twenty-five years ago we wouldn't have seen anything like John Edward or Sylvia Brown on television. During those times, when there were rules barring the use of the word "pregnant," the idea of communicating with a spirit would never have been broadcast to the masses. Certain practices associated with Spiritualism are common, everyday stuff now. Parapsychology courses are even taught in colleges today.

Warren was asked to give a lecture in a Comparative Religion class at Bethune Cookman College in Daytona Beach, Florida. The instructor told him prior to entering the classroom, "Do you know this is a Methodist school? You can expect anything." The instructor was warning Warren about the religious aspect of the college and telling him to expect rebuttal questions after his talk. However, the first question Warren was asked after the lecture was, "What do you think of astral projection?" The students had obviously been exposed to alternative thinking.

Warren and I were both interviewed by three students from Stetson University in DeLand, Florida, for a project they were doing for their Comparative Religion class. They were totally open to what we had to say, even agreeing with us on key points. Nothing we said shocked them during the interview.

Clairvoyance is a gift that adults frequently desire to develop, even though they may not have any recollection of having seen spirits as children. If they have not been compelled to do so earlier, it is common for people in their forties, fifties, and older to become interested in developing their psychic and spiritual abilities. When the desire occurs at this age, it is usually because the struggle for survival in the material world is at rest, says the Rev. Phoebe Rose Bergin. Usually people are secure enough with the material side of life by that age and are looking for more meaning, a more spiritual approach to life.

Those who have experienced clairvoyance during childhood sometimes retain this ability, as has been mentioned, but it is more common to lose the ability as we grow up. Yet, everyone is psychic. Yes, even you are psychic, right now, sitting in a chair or reading this passage in the aisle of a bookstore. Let's be real clear on this: Being psychic isn't mysterious—it's normal. When we instinctively know that it is our sister phoning, even though it is the wrong time of the day for her to call, we are exhibiting psychic abilities. When we start thinking about someone we haven't seen or heard from in years, and then we suddenly receive an e-mail from him or her later that evening, we are again exhibiting psychic abilities.

A medium, on the other hand, is a person whose sensitivities are such that he or she is able to be aware of and communicate with spirit entities. The communications received by Spiritualist mediums are believed to prove that there is a life hereafter. Those who practice meditation and, as followers of Spiritualism, seek to communicate with spirits believe that by communicating with the spirit world they are capable of bettering their lives by adhering to the wisdom received from spirits. However, all mediums are not necessarily Spiritualists.

Mediums see spirits, hear spirits, feel their presence, and can even smell them. All mediums are psychic, but not all psychics are mediums. Some people are born mediums, and others learn to develop mediumistic abilities. Both psychics and mediums are capable of possessing clairvoyant gifts. While psychics may not see spirits, they can see other things, such as objects, numbers, words, or scenes. Since everyone is psychic, everyone can be clairvoyant.

Because Arlene has so many experiences with spirits popping in or impressions from people, she spends a lot of time turning the switch off because she doesn't want to know other people's business. During a reading, she would rather be led in a manner that is helpful for the person. Arlene has no desire to interfere with another person's life outside of her office situation.

It's amusing to think about how many people get nervous around someone who is a professional psychic. They seem to think that psychics make a practice of standing around reading their minds, as if we have nothing better to do. What people don't realize is that their business is none of our concern and we aren't interested. After doing readings for clients, the last thing we want to do is zip into someone else's thoughts. It would be the same as if you work on computers all day at the office and then go home to find that a neighbor wants you to look at his computer. You probably wouldn't want to do it.

As mediums, it is important for us to learn how to turn off our clairvoyant abilities because, otherwise, we would be bombarded with unwanted energies all the time. When asked whether I turn off my abilities, I always give the hypothetical example of being "on" and then walking through the local mall. My antennae would be going crazy receiving every vibration around! In the case of an emergency, or if we are otherwise occupied, our ability is always there when we need it. Sometimes when Carol is vacuuming her house, she will hear the spirits talking to her when it is necessary to get a message across.

There are times when urgent circumstances bring about clairvoyance or enhance the existing ability, such as when a near-death experience intensified Carol's interests and abilities. After Carol delivered her son, she almost died. While Carol was slipping away, the nurse, also a young woman, compassionately held Carol's hand and cried. Carol noticed the nurse crying after she left her body. She asked God to let her come back so she could tell the nurse to stop crying, and that she was okay. This request was granted and Carol returned to her body, where she remained. After that near-death experience, everything changed for Carol. She felt very different. She didn't speak about the near-death experience for years, but she studied and read books about this phenomena so she could understand what had happened (and was happening) to her.

Trauma can make a person "wake up and wise up," according to Arlene. Sudden traumatic events can be a catalyst to our discovery of the spiritual realm. We can suddenly have enhanced abilities after we suffer a trauma, such as was the case with Carol after her near-death experience. Dannion Brinkley wrote an entire book about a traumatic experience that suddenly propelled him into a spiritual realm. In his book *Saved by the Light*, Dannion writes about how he was talking on the telephone to a friend while a thunderstorm was approaching. Although Dannion suggested hanging up, his friend did not want to end the conversation. Suddenly, Dannion was struck by lightning. The heat from the strike was so intense that it melted the phone into his hand and glued the nails in his shoes to the flooring nails. His body was flung over the bed, minus his shoes.

Dannion then had an out-of-body experience. He saw his wife giving him cardiopulmonary resuscitation, and he saw the friend with whom he had been talking on the phone rush through the door. Apparently the friend had heard the boom over the phone. Dannion watched all of this from above.

Dannion experienced himself going into his body and back out again prior to being transported to the emergency room by ambulance. During the ride to the hospital, Dannion was pronounced dead. Once they arrived at the hospital, the staff in the emergency room did all they could to revive Dannion, but nothing worked. During this time of attempted resuscitation, Dannion's spirit was in a place he would later call the Crystal City, where he was visiting with Beings of Light.

While all these dramatic rescue attempts were taking place, it was determined in the Crystal City, as Dannion later wrote, that he had a mission to perform on earth and that he would have to return to his physical body. And so he did. But along with his return, he brought an ability to accurately read minds and make predictions of future world events. His life was irrevocably changed forever.

We do not have to experience a traumatic event in order to develop clairvoyance. No one would want to suffer the pain Dannion experienced for years during his recovery or risk dying to expedite his or her abilities. Subjective clairvoyance is not difficult to develop, especially if you happen to be a naturally visual person. Those who can follow a guided meditation exercise and easily see what they are being directed to visualize should be able to develop subjective clairvoyance without any difficulty. The more challenging part comes when we try to interpret what we are seeing in meditation in order to make sense of what we are being shown.

We can all certainly learn to enhance any natural clairvoyant abilities we possess or cultivate the ability of subjective clairvoyance if we have that desire. Possibly we can develop objective clairvoyance. Patience and practice, plus a good teacher, is all you need to develop clairvoyance.

three

Meditation First

If spiritual growth has become important to you or you have a desire to be more in tune with nature and all things that are psychic, you will be required to devote your time and energy to this endeavor. For this dedication, you will be rewarded with a life that will be forever changed for the better. Carol, who has been teaching clairvoyance classes for over twenty years, claims that with practice, everyone can develop clairvoyance. I second that claim. We can all develop clairvoyance if our hearts and intentions are sincere.

Whether your goal is to develop clairvoyance or enhance the natural clairvoyant abilities that you possess, you need to allot time for daily meditation. Therefore, Carol's recommendation for developing clairvoyance is this: meditation, meditation, meditation. The reason meditation is essential for development is because it is through meditation that we start to develop our psychic and/or mediumistic talents. Arlene agrees that meditation is essential. She believes we must be in a "wholeness place of body, mind, and spirit—a peaceful, resonate space, so that a connection is made with the higher power. That way we know we are in sync."

Arlene says that it is important to recognize a process in order to get in tune. This requires that we be in a place of receptivity with the Infinite. This place of receptivity is achieved through meditation. The preferred process to develop clairvoyance is through daily, private meditation, and working with a meditation group under the tutelage of a medium.

Our intention is also an important factor in achieving development of clairvoyance. Meditation is not a game or a practice one should desire to learn just so he or she can "psyche" in on someone. Both Carol and Warren believe that to be successful we must have the right intention, sincerity, and be willing to really dedicate ourselves to the work of developing our spiritual gifts. After all, to haphazardly do anything in life is not acceptable, especially when it is something as serious as developing spiritual abilities. This is important business, which should not be taken lightly.

We've all heard the saying, "How do you get to Carnegie Hall? Practice, practice, practice." This is so true! We can't learn to play the piano unless we practice. Dancing may come naturally for some, but without practice, opportunities for advancement are limited. We can't learn to speak another language unless we devote practice time to that objective. Tiger Woods did not become a phenomenon in golf with his good looks. He *practiced*.

Select a time for your meditation when you will not be disturbed. This may take some effort on your part to arrange, and some practice for other members in the household. I always recommend posting a Do Not Disturb sign on the door so others know that when the door is closed and the sign is up, you are to be left alone. You deserve this time to yourself, so insist that you receive it. With tongue in cheek, I always advise people to tell the rest of the family, "Unless the house is on fire, don't bother me!"

Meditation doesn't have to last hours, or even a half hour. Fifteen minutes is all that is necessary—ten minutes if you're rushed. Choose a time that is far enough past a meal so you aren't sleepy, and a time when you can be consistent; for example, don't meditate at 10 a.m. on Saturday mornings unless you can meditate at 10 a.m. during the week also.

Many mediums suggest meditating at eight o'clock at night. When I attended development classes, 8 p.m. always seemed to be when we began meditation, or shortly thereafter. This time works well for most folks because it falls far enough past dinnertime to be conducive to your tummy's digestion. It is not good to have an overly-stuffed tummy when meditating. If you happen to work at night, an evening meditation would not be the ideal time for you. In this case, you will have to experiment to find the time that is appropriate for you.

Once you establish the best time, keep the date. It's called "keeping a date with spirit." If you aren't consistent, the spirits won't be, either. Haphazard meditation does not work. Consistency does. We could liken it to learning to play the piano. If you only sit in front of the keyboard occasionally, you won't develop much as a pianist, will you? Daily practice is what accomplishes the goal when learning how to play the piano *and* learning how to be clairvoyant.

Get a chair that is comfortable, but not too comfortable. If you use a recliner, you might as well crawl into bed! The idea is to be comfortable, but attentive. A straight-backed chair that is cushioned would do nicely. Many dining room chairs are perfect for meditation.

Some people like to "set the mood." By this, I mean they light candles and burn incense. These two actions are commonly used during meditation; they are triggers that tell our brains that it's time to meditate. Some of us may want to add items to enhance the ambiance. If you have read any of my other books, you will have noticed that I suggest the use of altars. Establishing an altar that you will meditate in front of is a good practice and can only help to assist you in the meditation process. Automatically, you know when you come before your altar, it's time to meditate.

Once you have chosen a proper chair in which to sit, close your eyes and listen to a guided meditation tape or CD. Note that I'm not suggesting that you sit or lie on the floor. There are no benefits to either for a person beginning meditation. The reason I advise using a guided meditation rather than soft music is because the most frequent complaint I hear from people learning to meditate is, "My mind is too busy." They can't still the mind chatter long enough to receive a satisfactory experience. Thoughts of going to the grocery store, what will happen at the office the next day, and how the children are misbehaving keep dancing through their brains. Give your mind something to do by providing it with a guided meditation to follow.

Guided imagery is key to getting us to that place of receptivity, and it is essential in the development of clairvoyance. Teachers believe in the importance of guided meditations because, in the words of Arlene, "This will lead you to a connection with your higher power so that you know you are in sync with that higher power." Let's not forget that the information we receive during meditation comes through the Infinite.

Group energy is another valuable tool that can help development. A very special unity can be formed when people are developing together. We experience the unfolding of each other's spiritual abilities, which is a unique process to enjoy together. Join a psychic or spiritual development class that is being conducted by a reputable medium or psychic.

The additional value here is that the teacher will be able to observe you and give you input to further your advancement. Also, you will have a better experience because the group is working with a collective energy. During my development days I remember feeling like I was being recharged during the class. As the week wore on, it seemed like my psychic energy waned during my private meditations. I couldn't wait to return to class to receive another boost of spiritual energy!

Another advantage to a group encounter is that we can learn from each other. What one person experiences, you, too, will experience eventually. Observe how the more advanced students handle themselves. Listen to how the teacher guides an exercise where he or she directs the students to extract more information during a message. Through observation of others and with the teacher's assistance, we learn to discern whether or not it is truth or our imagination that is being shown to us during meditation.

When joining with a group it's important to feel comfortable with and enlightened by the people. When we're opening, we want to open into light, not someone else's "stuff." When trying to develop, there is nothing worse than having a psychic drain or a negative person in the group. His or her energy will pull down the entire group. Don't accept a lesser vibration, because as we unfold, we become more sensitive. If a person isn't stable, for instance, he or she could go off on a tangent and see or feel something that is, in reality, an overactive imagination, or he or she may even have a paranoid experience. If you find yourself in a situation like that, speak to other students and the teacher to validate your concern. The teacher should ask the one with the offending energy to leave the class. If the teacher does not, then remove yourself and seek another teacher. You're in the wrong class.

Sometimes a beginning student is unable to really see much of anything at first, even when being directed during a guided meditation. So, what do you do if you close your eyes, listen to the instructions, and you just can't see anything? Simple: keep practicing. Rome wasn't built in a day, as they say, and clairvoyance won't be achieved overnight, either. It will come. Give it time, and give yourself a break; you're learning. Everyone develops at his or her own pace. Some of the exercises in this book will come naturally, others will take more practice, and a few will be difficult. Don't set yourself up for disappointment by creating expectations. Don't expect anything, and something will happen!

On the other hand, many times we don't realize we are seeing. Warren said he has had students who voiced discouragement and were upset because they didn't see anything during his guided meditation. When this would occur, Warren would sit them down and talk to them. He asked them if they ever saw light or clouds pass in front of their eyes when they were falling asleep. They said yes. As it turned out, the students were looking for something more spectacular than light or clouds, and didn't realize that they were actually *seeing*.

Frequently, colors are one of the very first things a student begins to see. A student will often say he or she saw a screen of color covering the total area behind the eyelids, or spots of color, which are called "spirit lights." That's a beginning! It's happening! You could look at it this way: you're warming up.

Not everyone is gregarious and self-confident. When a student is shy or lacks confidence, he or she creates a stumbling block: fear. After all, no one wants to appear foolish when delivering a message or an impression. And certainly no one wants to fail to receive. Receiving nothing will make a student appear foolish or inept. Thus, some students are hesitant to publicly make any predictions or claims of a spirit presence, so they allow fear to shut down their abilities.

We all have to start somewhere. The first lesson on the piano isn't usually a glorious experience, either. But with practice, results begin to be heard. Eventually, we are playing the scales, then a short tune. With time and patience, messages will be received and interpreted correctly, too. Don't allow fear to block your desired path. After all, the best student in your class had to start somewhere.

The ability to see spirit lights is a very normal occurrence, and it never leaves us. During the course of any day, it is not unusual at all to see flashes of blue out of the corners of our eyes, or even a quick blink of blue across the page of the book we are reading. We might see a blue light next to the head of someone with whom we are talking. It could be likened to seeing a firefly suddenly light up and then extinguish. There it is . . . and poof! Now it's gone.

Spirit lights can come in other colors besides blue. Sometimes the lights are white, pink, green, or purple, depending on how the spirit decides to work. The lights may appear in a cluster or there may be only one light. The Rev. Arlene Sikora sees lights when she does readings for clients. This is how Arlene's guiding forces have chosen to let her know they are present. The lights will appear around or over the client's head, separate from his or her aura. The individually colored lights come through in the colors of turquoise, purple, cobalt blue, and white. At times the spirit lights will blend together. Arlene says that when this happens, the counsel is talking. The counsel, she explains, is a group energy, a master force, a collective consciousness. In other words, it's powerful.

Sometimes Arlene sees words accompanied by sound. By combining sound, the word "stop" could be seen and heard in a very direct manner to indicate cease and desist immediately. Usually when you receive a warning word combined with a sound, it is an indication of something very important. When commands or warnings are received more than once, pay attention *now* because this is an important message being delivered. You will learn that the Universe has interesting ways of getting our attention so that we avoid unfortunate events. Remember Phoebe's husband, Bill, and the tire?

A medium who once lived in Cassadaga was sitting in her living room, quietly reading. Suddenly, she heard a voice shout, "Run!" Not one to question a spirit, she immediately got up from her chair and ran to the front door. As she approached the door, she heard a crash from behind. When she turned around she saw that a huge tree limb had fallen through the roof of her house, landing over the chair she had been occupying.

Recently I spoke at a Unitarian Universalist church in Orlando, and a gentleman from the congregation shared a story with me. He said that recently he had been at an intersection waiting for the light to turn green. It was his habit to accelerate immediately after the light changed from red to green, but on this particular day, he did not hasten. He heard a voice clearly say, "Don't move out when the light is green. Wait." No one was with him in the car at the time. Nevertheless, the man obeyed the command. As he sat still in his car with the green light glowing in front of him, another car came tearing across the intersection. The car surely would have struck his car and caused him serious injury, and, quite possibly, death.

Since we are all individuals, we cannot expect any one method to work for all of us. What may not work for you will work for another, and it may take a little trial and error to find a method that works for you. Just be consistent with your meditation, and have patience. The information you gain from reading this book should give you a good idea of what to anticipate during meditation.

The rest of this book has exercises at the end of each chapter. It is set up to be a workbook so you can record your experiences. However, it is important to eventually purchase a journal or set up a file on your computer so you can record information and experiences that are received during meditations and your daily life. Be sure to date every entry in this workbook and in your journal. We are only human, so there is no way we are going to remember everything. The most seemingly minor impression you save in your workbook or journal could become very significant when you review it in the future. We often are surprised when we refer back to our previous recordings and see a pattern or recognize something that made absolutely no sense at the time it was received. Sometimes messages are shown only once, while others are repeated.

If you happen to receive a symbol, for instance, you may not consider it to be important. Later, it could gain significance once you have established a way to interpret your own personal symbols. Chapter 5 is devoted entirely to symbols, and you will find that chapter to be very helpful.

It is also important to record experiences that you have outside of meditation. Meditation is not the only way we receive information. As we go about our daily lives, impressions are given to us and intuition is received. We may be driving a car and receive an impression when we look at a road sign. Sometimes we experience an unexplained urge that requires our attention, or our normal way of receiving may change. These are important events to record.

The messages we receive have a purpose, and they teach us lessons in awareness. Phoebe found that one of the hardest things for her to learn was to rely on faith. One night when she was preparing to return home from doing group readings in someone's house, one of the ladies asked Phoebe to stay for coffee and cake. Phoebe really didn't have any reason to hurry home, but politely declined the offer anyway. The woman persisted, tempting Phoebe with an offer of chocolate cake. "Well," Phoebe thought, "I can't pass up chocolate cake!" As it turned out, it was a good thing Phoebe had not driven home directly after the readings were performed. When Phoebe finally left for home, upon approaching the highway closest to Cassadaga, she saw two ambulances, three fire engines, and all kinds of police cars at the corner. Phoebe realized that she could very well have been involved in some sort of accident had she left when she originally had planned.

Many times we will delay our travels somewhere, be compelled to look at another countertop at a home improvement store, or try on another pair of shoes at a department store. Later, we find out some terrible accident occurred that we could have been involved in if we hadn't taken another path. This could be called Divine Intervention or seen as protection of some sort coming from the Universe or our spiritual teachers. The message is that we are being watched over. These are important experiences to record. Also, be sure to write down when you *don't* listen—those times when something happens and you think, "I had a feeling I shouldn't do this! Why didn't I listen?" Be sure to record all of these experiences in your journal. They are important to your development because they will teach you to have faith in your guidance and to be more aware.

My very first teacher was a wonderful medium named Ruth Callin. Ruth always told her students a little story about how she was instructed to see clairvoyantly. Ruth's teacher, who happened to be her mother-in-law, taught the old-fashioned way: she told Ruth to sit alone in the corner of a dark room every night and stare into the corner until she saw something. I believe Ruth said it took a year before she ever saw anything, and, at best, it was a light!

I have found that most people do not like to meditate in a pitch-black room—a room so dark you can't see your hand before your face. I know I don't enjoy it. I find it to be a handicap. Warren mentioned that years ago it was a common practice to teach development classes in a very dark room so students would not be distracted by other students or feel that they were being watched. When Warren started his training at Camp Silver Bell, in Ephrata, Pennsylvania, the students were placed in total darkness. Eventually, the light would be increased until the students became accustomed to more light and could give messages in sunlight. Most people do not teach the old-fashioned method anymore. Results can easily be obtained in a darkened room with one candle lit. This is a comfortable atmosphere in which to meditate and works well for everyone.

A Simple Meditation Exercise follows. Please use the basic instructions in this exercise for all the exercises, unless something else is suggested. Those who are practiced in meditation may find this section too easy. If that is the case, utilize these exercises as a test of your ability to focus.

Simple Meditation Exercise

Go to that special, quiet area in your home that allows for freedom from distractions. Many people enjoy listening to soft music while meditating, especially in the beginning stages. It helps to drown out any unavoidable noise, such as garbage trucks and sirens. Once you finish with the beginning stage of meditation in this chapter, you can use guided meditation tapes.

Sit in your comfortable (but not too comfortable) chair. Sit in a position with your feet flat on the floor. Do not cross your ankles or knees. Allow your hands to rest easily in your lap, with the palms facing upward. Close your eyes. Now, breathe in deeply, hold the breath a few seconds, and exhale. Repeat this two more times. Tilt your head to the right and then left, then backward and forward. Shrug your shoulders, then tense your arms and hands, and release. Flex your shoulders backward and forward, then release. Tighten the buttocks area, release, then tighten the thighs, calves, and feet, releasing each afterward. Take in another deep breath. At this point your body should be sufficiently relaxed. Sometimes we think we are relaxed until we tense our body and discover that we are tight. Tightening and releasing various areas ensures that your body is truly relaxed and helps to produce a successful meditation. As you continue to practice meditation, you can skip the physical tightening and releasing, as it will become unnecessary.

Once your body is relaxed, focus your closed eyes slightly upward. This will help to put you in the alpha state. What you are seeing is your "screen" on which you will view clairvoyant impressions. At first it will be dark, like you are looking at the back of your eyelids—which you are! With time it will change and you will learn to change the color. If at any point your concentration strays during an exercise, simply focus your attention on your breath. Pay attention as you slowly breathe in and out, then return to the exercise. Many people use this breathing focus as their main instrument to become relaxed.

Once you have completed an exercise, breathe deliberately. Focus on your breathing, and then start to pay attention to your body, the chair underneath you, and your surroundings. When you are attentive to your surroundings, open your eyes.

EXERCISE 1

Focus your mind on your viewing screen. Imagine the screen turning to white or blue, so that all that is within your inner vision is either white or blue. If another color pops into your view instead, that's okay. The purpose is to imagine a color. Once you have seen one color, change the screen to a different color. Keep changing the colors until you are able to visualize red, orange, yellow, blue, green, indigo, and then purple. This may be an easy exercise and you will be able to visualize all the colors the first time, or it may take several attempts. Pat yourself on the back for a job well done! Record your experience in the Workbook section in this book (page 145).

EXERCISE 2

Become relaxed (as described in the Simple Meditation Exercise, page 48). Focus your attention on your inner vision screen. See if you can visualize the screen as being white. On the screen, imagine a square block. Whatever color the block appears, change it to another color, and then keep changing the color. Continue with this exercise by imagining a triangle, a circle, and a rectangle individually, each time changing the color it first appears into other colors. Next, change the color of the background behind the shapes and the colors of the shapes. Play with this for a while. Record your experience in the Workbook.

Exercise 3

After relaxing, focus on your inner screen. Visualize a familiar room in your house, other than the one you are in. This could be a special room, such as your library or bedroom. It could also be a communal room, such as the living room or kitchen. Observe the four corners of the room. Pay attention to all the accoutrements present. What colors are visible to your inner eyes? What fixtures, furniture, or appliances are in this room? What objects do you see? What paintings or other decorative items are hanging on the walls? What does the flooring look like? Record your experience in the Workbook.

EXERCISE 4

Become relaxed. Visualize a place in nature, such as a beach scene, a mountainous area, the forest, or a peaceful lake. Go into this scene as much as possible. Become one with nature. See everything in great detail. Look at the ground, up at the sky, and all points in between. What colors are present? Touch the grains of sand, rocky edges, tree bark, foliage, and/or water substance present. *Feel* these things. Notice the texture, notice the temperature. Is there an odor associated with this scene? Flowers have a scent, as do trees and snow. What do you smell? Be sure to record your experience in the Workbook.

four

Interpretation

At least two abilities are necessary in order to interpret what we receive clairvoyantly, although we may be fortunate enough to develop more than two. Besides clairvoyance, the other abilities that we may experience are *clairaudience,* which is a French word meaning "clear hearing"; *clairgustance*, which means "clear smelling"; and *clairsentience*, which means "clear sensing." When we are first developing our spiritual talents, we may actually do more sensing before we see anything significant through clairvoyance. Every professional medium and psychic has clairsentient abilities, and it is through clairsentience that we interpret many things we see clairvoyantly. With our keener, natural intuition at play, we may feel the answer to a question prior to actually being able to see any images during meditation.

It is an intuitive gift, to sense. In our normal lives, we often receive feelings. Some people might call this "women's intuition," but men are capable of sensing equally as well. Have you ever watched a police show on television where a detective will say that he has a hunch? That's intuition. Anyone, male or female, could be shopping in a downtown area and suddenly be faced with the decision to either take a shortcut through an alley or a longer route down several streets. He or she may sense that the alley is unsafe, even though the neighborhood appears to be good. The person heeds the intuitive part of his or her being and chooses to take the longer way home. That's an example of paying attention to our intuitive sense.

Once we start receiving images, it is very natural for us to react to the images presented to us through feelings. For instance, if we were to describe a gentleman in spirit as having whitish hair, a slender build, and a smirk on his face, we would interpret our observations by how the image makes us feel. Based on his appearance, our feelings might suggest to us that the man is older than he really is, and that he has a quirky personality. When we *see* something, we *feel* something in association with what we see. That's clairsentience. Remember, it takes two abilities to interpret impressions. Therefore, it is very important to pay attention to how you *feel* during meditation. Many cues will be received by your senses that will help you interpret what you see.

I remember one of my teachers asking us to pay attention to how we felt within our bodies when we were accurate. Usually, something occurs that is noticeable, or a sensation is felt. For me it has always been a sensation in my head. I'm not sure I would describe it as a physical sensation, but something happens inside my head. It's that lightbulb moment, or, like Oprah says, that "aha!" moment.

The point my teacher was making was to remember how it felt to be accurate. By referring back to that feeling, we compare it to how we presently feel about another situation. Are the feelings the same? If not, we're probably not going to be accurate in our assessment or prediction.

For Arlene, there is a strong knowingness that is present when she recognizes that she is "on." However, for some of us, when we are accurate the feeling can be subtle. When in meditation, what we are seeing may appear obvious, but the key to accuracy is the interpretation of what we are seeing. No psychic or medium is totally right all the time. After all, we are human beings and subject to misinterpreting what we see or feel. Most of our inaccurate statements come from the human error factor of interpretation.

"You give what you get and it just feels right. However, you don't know beyond a shadow of a doubt that you are truly accurate," Arlene says. But then there are those wonderful times when Arlene receives confirmation from the client. One client in particular exclaimed, "Holy _____ ! That's amazing!" So, pay close attention to how you feel when receiving impressions clairvoyantly so you can recognize when you are accurate.

Now, you are probably thinking that the other person will confirm your accuracy. Not necessarily so! There are times when a person does not want to accept the information we give. The person may be in a state of denial or simply doesn't comprehend what we are saying. Also, sometimes people do not know the spirit entity we bring through from the spirit side. For example, often a person never knew his or her grandparents. If this happens, the person will have to ask someone who *did* know the grandparents if the description was accurate. We aren't necessarily inaccurate, but we certainly cannot anticipate receiving confirmation from a person who cannot face reality or identify a spirit. So, learn how you *feel* when you are accurate.

Also, during your private meditations there will be no one to confirm your accuracy. As far as how to proceed, you will have to rely on your feelings. When the final results occur, you will receive the confirmation. In either case, be sure to record how you felt in your journal.

We are all individuals, so we are going to receive impressions differently. One person may see symbols, while another will receive nothing along those lines. One may see only in black and white, while another will view full-color images. How we approach receiving images can also vary.

Phoebe sees subjective colors, scenes, and people, but rarely does she see symbols. During a reading, she prefers to have her eyes closed so that she is not influenced by the client's reactions. With her eyes closed, Phoebe's concentration is totally on what she is seeing clairvoyantly; therefore, she is better able to interpret what she sees. Not all mediums and psychics work with their eyes closed, but this is how Phoebe is most comfortable. This method may or may not appeal to you.

Arlene says that sometimes what she sees is solid, but other times it is within the mind consciousness. She sees colors, symbols, scenes, and faces of people, and sometimes what she sees is like a moving film, going from one scene to another. This is what Arlene interprets as a progression of what is about to happen in a client's life. During these scenes, she is also hearing words rather than seeing them.

I see faces, scenes, symbols, colors, and words subjectively during a reading. Some mediums see words more often than others. To convey the message to me, sometimes a spirit will give me a word to read. The way a spirit chooses to show the word is to have it appear across the person or above his or her head when my eyes are open. When a word appears this way, I am not literally seeing a word forming in the air; I am seeing it in my mind's eye while looking at someone or something. The word usually appears white as it crosses whatever is in my line of vision. Words may appear in a different manner to other mediums, but this way is the most common manner of appearance.

The word I am receiving may be a sign of a person's personality, or it may be an answer to a question. If I am describing a person's personality, I may see the word "cautious." This tells me that the person is a careful individual who is not spontaneous or prone to making hasty decisions. If a client asks, "What month do you see me taking a vacation this year?" and the word "May" flashes in my thoughts, then that's the answer: May.

Numbers are commonly seen in our inner vision and can be a very expressive means to convey a message. No, not lottery numbers! If lottery numbers came to us in meditation, all mediums would be rich! In response to a question, we are more likely to receive house numbers, a birth date, or a singular number to indicate a length of time. For instance, a man who has been out of work may want to know how much longer he will remain unemployed. The number three could flash into the medium's vision and she could *feel* that it means three weeks. So, the answer would be three weeks.

Jim loves to work with numbers. Sometimes when working in this manner he is talking about house numbers. Once when Jim was delivering a set of numbers to a client, he described a woman associated with the numbers. A bitter taste came into Jim's mouth, so he described the situation between the client and this woman as bitter. As it turned out, the client stated that she did have a bitter relationship with the woman. The client was able to identify her mortal enemy from this interpretation of the message.

As mediums, many times we see a scene or a symbol and do not know how it applies to our client. Frankly, it's really none of our business, anyway. It is not necessary for us to understand the meaning; it is only necessary for the client to understand. After all, the message is for the client. Sometimes what we say sounds strange to us, but if the client is smiling and nodding, we know what we're saying is making sense to him or her, which is all that matters.

Phoebe says she has learned to go with what she receives even when it appears crazy. She will be thinking, "What are they (the spirits) giving me now?" But she still relays what she is seeing. During times like these Phoebe will either receive a hearty laugh from her client, or what she says will floor him or her. For instance, one time Phoebe was reading for a very heavy woman. The first visual Phoebe received was a whale. She even saw the blowhole spurting water. Phoebe thought, "I can't tell her this!" The image stayed with her, as if spirit were trying to tell Phoebe, "This is it. Say it." Phoebe relented, saying without any apologies, "I'm seeing this large whale and he's right in front of you. As far as the blowhole, the water is going up through the spout."

The client started to laugh and said, "It's my husband in spirit. I love the water and whenever we were out in the water he used to call me his little whale because I used to lay on my back and blow water." Now you understand why Phoebe always trusts what she receives, no matter how peculiar it appears to her. After all, it only has to make sense to the client. Therefore, give what you get, regardless of the seeming absurdity.

When Carol is doing a reading, she sees pictures and scenes associated with the client's life. She will see and hear inside her head and outside her inner hearing, as she explains it. Sometimes Carol feels through her whole body, and other times, outside of her body. She views the scene like it's a play being acted out inside her head, then uses her senses and clairaudient ability to interpret what she is seeing clairvoyantly.

If a woman is having a problem with her spouse, for example, Carol, in her mind, will place the spouse beside the client and have them face each other. Then she observes how they interact with each other, like a pantomime. Carol then asks the figures in her inner vision questions and receives verbal answers. Sometimes they will continue to act out in pantomime. Carol tells the client what is happening, then senses what is going on and tells the client what her interpretation is of the scene. Carol will do this exercise with her eyes open or closed, depending on what she feels is most suitable.

Carol's visual pictures are very clear when she knows she is "on." The same is true with sound—when it's very sharp, she knows she's accurate. When Carol is inaccurate, it is because she has interpreted incorrectly. There are also times when Carol will struggle to interpret something because she feels the client's fears are blocking the interpretation. Other times it is Carol's fears that block an interpretation. You see, Carol is a sensitive, caring person, and does not want to bring up things that will disturb or possibly hurt the client. When she allows her fears to get in the way, she is blocked.

Colors—usually the first thing we see as a beginner—are normally followed by objects and items. We may see a child's scooter, a cat, a house, a locket, or anything else you can name. Let's suppose that during a development class one student states that he saw a tree house associated with another individual in class. The other individual may relate the tree house to his childhood, or perhaps has been thinking about building a tree house for his son. Whatever the case, that would be a confirmation of accuracy. As the student's development progresses, he would be able to sense that the tree house is from childhood or that the individual is currently thinking of building or actually *is* building a tree house. The student would simply feel it. No pictures are involved; it is a *feeling*.

Spirits are seen within the inner vision of individuals who are sensitive to that energy. This may happen early or it may take a little time to develop. Each person develops at a different rate because of his or her individual sensitivity and dedication, so no one can state with certainty when spirits will be viewed within the inner vision. I saw spirits and scenes within my inner vision immediately, but I am a very visual person. One who is less visual may have to work longer at seeing; however, this person may hear quickly. A more visual person may never hear a spirit. Everything depends on individuality.

Warren has found over the years of doing readings that if he sees the spirit standing by the client, he knows that the spirit is for the client, not himself. It is not one of his guides. The clients are the ones who bring the spirits with them to a reading, not the medium. Many people think it's the opposite, and that we, the mediums, conjure up the spirits, bidding them to attend the readings. But spirits cannot be compelled to visit us. There is a psychic vibration that accompanies the client, and along with that vibration travels the spirits that wish to communicate.

Once we start seeing spirits, we may receive some unusual images. A hand may come into our psychic vision, a singular face, or just an upper torso. Other times we may see a full figure. There is no way to predict how the spirits will choose to manifest into your vision. In the case of manifestations, a spirit's appearance is entirely up to that spirit.

When giving a reading and receiving an impression of a spirit, it is common for a medium to see a piece of jewelry flash in his or her mind. This is one way that a spirit will try to convey identification. This particular jewelry item would have significance to the spirit in question or to the person receiving the reading. For instance, a broach with blue stones could be a piece of jewelry that a deceased grandmother used to wear, or it could have been a present she gave to her granddaughter prior to her passing.

Spirits will also use objects associated with them to help mediums identify them to a client. A good example would be the time I saw a woman in spirit playing a bagpipe. The odd part about the bagpipe-playing spirit is that she was dressed in a babushka. A woman dressed in a babushka playing a bagpipe? How absurd! My interpretation came from *feeling* that this woman did not speak English, and I observed that she was from a Middle Eastern country be-cause of her garb. Even though the woman sitting in front of me was as Middle Eastern in her appearance as a ballet slipper, this made perfect sense to her. Her great aunt had played several instruments, including the bagpipe, in a mu-sical group. The great aunt did not speak English, and she was from the Middle East. For the woman receiving the reading, the bagpipe was a significant object that clearly identified the spirit.

As a rule, your first impression is the one to give out. Every teacher with whom I have studied and every teacher I know today advises, "Give your first thought." If we de-liberate on the impression, our conscious mind steps in to analyze the situation. Once that happens, we have removed ourselves from being objective observers. From then on we are allowing our rational mind to do the work. We are no longer in the flow with spirit.

It takes a brave soul to relay his or her impressions. No one enjoys being wrong, and we do risk that perception when we give our interpretations. However, we should not feel that we must be right. Instead, we should attempt to be accurate. By attempting to be accurate, we remove the right and wrong in the situation. Professional mediums receive seemingly bizarre impressions, as noted previously, so it is safe to presume that students will receive equally bizarre images. It's quite normal for students to be hesitant to express what they see in their inner vision, especially when what they see is really goofy. But interpretation is key, as is practice. With enough practice, we will learn how to accurately interpret what we see.

"Why didn't you give a message tonight?" I asked one of my best students after class.

"All I saw was a woman holding a tuba. That was too peculiar," the student expressed to me. "It wasn't right. I must have been off, so I didn't want to say anything that dumb."

I told the student that because she had not shared the impression of the woman holding a tuba, one person did not receive a communication from her aunt in spirit. I happened to know that one woman in the circle that night had a dear aunt in spirit who used to play the tuba for a living. This particular aunt was very special to the woman because she had raised her as her own daughter.

Please realize that many of the impressions we receive are not going to make any sense to us at all, as I clearly stated in previous examples. The whole point is whether or not it makes sense to the other person. If so, then we are accurate. *Give your first impression*, no matter how dumb it appears!

When we first start practicing to see images, we are doing so with our eyes closed during meditation. After all, it is common to meditate with the eyes closed, although there are other forms of meditation that are done with the eyes open, such as a walking meditation. It seems easier to receive and interpret images with the eyes closed. We aren't bothered by distractions because we are blocking out sight. Eventually, though, most people are able to see clairvoyantly with their eyes wide open. Such instances may occur when staring out into the backyard while doing the dishes. Washing dishes can be very meditative, and many people receive impressions while doing this. Even while driving a car I will receive impressions. Perhaps your special time will be while you are taking a shower.

Mediums often demonstrate their abilities at message services, and they do so with their eyes wide open. A message service is usually conducted at a Spiritualist church, and the public is invited to come so they can receive messages from spirits. During these services, it is common to hear mediums say such things as, "I see a woman standing behind you," "I see the number three over your head," or "This spirit is handing you a rose."

The mediums aren't literally seeing the spirit, the number, or the gift, in most cases. These are expressions that we are taught to use when delivering messages from spirits. What the medium is actually seeing is something in his or her inner vision that is intended to identify the spirit. The rose, for example, may have been a grandmother's favorite flower, so the spirit giving a rose to the person would be significant.

Spontaneous clairvoyance is common among mediums. This is an occurrence where a spirit will appear outside of meditation and without a person having any conscious desire to see a spirit. One night Warren was at his computer surfing the Internet when he heard a spirit knocking on his door. Warren said, "Come in and sit down." The spirit did. Warren said it was a spirit just passing through, not a relative of his or anyone he recognized.

Every once in a while Warren sees a particular spirit walking about the hallway of Brigham Hall, the small apartment building in which he lives. Warren believes the spirit is Dr. Sarah Brigham because of the way she is dressed. The spirit wears a long dress with ruffles, and she appears quite prim and dignified. During the early establishment of Cassadaga, a married couple, Drs. Hubbard and Sarah Brigham, both eclectic physicians, built the apartment house in 1896. It is likely that Warren is seeing the spirit of Dr. Sarah Brigham.

As we develop, it is important for us to be very aware. In order for a spirit to be recognized, we must describe the visual we are receiving in a way that a client can identify the spirit. General descriptions are not helpful. After all, a medium-tall man with gray hair who is wearing blue shorts would describe half the men in Florida. We have to be more specific. In early development, it is common to leave out pertinent information. We see it, but we aren't describing it. It's as if we assume that everyone else is seeing what we are seeing. Upon closer examination, we could say, "The man is slight in weight, walks with difficulty at times, does not express his pain to others, and he likes to wear flashy ties when he dresses up." The interpretation of "does not express his pain to others" comes from observation and using the additional ability of clairsentience. Therefore, it is important to feel and *observe* when interpreting.

Diane used to train her students to be observant and aware by asking them questions when they entered the room for class.

"What color was the doormat?"

"Did you notice any cats on the porch when you entered?"

"Close your eyes. What color is Jack's shirt?"

It was amazing to realize how many objects and colors the students did not observe. To help your development, it pays to be aware in your daily life. Here are some exercises that will help you with observation and concentration, and eventually assist you with your interpretations.

Observation Exercises

EXERCISE 1

Think back to the last time you entered a bank, a store, the grocery, or a post office. What do you remember observing when you were in there? Were there a lot of people? Were they different ethnicities or were they all pretty much the same? What colors stand out? Describe the person who waited on you. What was the person wearing? What color was his or her hair? Estimate the age of the person. Did he or she wear jewelry? Were his or her ears pierced? Write down your experiences in the Workbook (page 145).

The next time you enter that place, be observant. Pay attention to color, people, clothing, attitudes, and small details.

Exercise 2

After riding home on a commuter train, describe the people who were on the train with you. Try to remember every detail, and record your experiences in the Workbook.

Exercise 3

While sitting in a doctor's office, a beauty salon, or riding the bus, observe the appearance of the other patrons. How would you describe these people to a police officer if a crime had been committed? While you wait, construct that description.

Practice being observant everywhere you go from now on. When you return home, write down the results in the Workbook.

Concentration Exercises

EXERCISE 1

Select an object, such as a candle in a candlestick holder. Light the candle and examine it closely. Let the image saturate your mind. You will find that other thoughts begin to enter into your consciousness. This is a natural occurrence. Gently push them aside and return to concentrating on the candle. After about three minutes, close your eyes and visualize the candle. Hold the image continually in your mind. If other thoughts creep in, push them gently aside as before. If the image fades, open your eyes and view the candle again, then close your eyes and continue visualizing it. The same exercise can be performed using a colorful cup, a stuffed animal, a flower, or a small statue. Repeat this exercise daily for at least a week. Record your successes in the Workbook each time.

EXERCISE 2

Select someone you know very well, preferably someone with whom you live. Close your eyes and visualize this person's face. See the face as clearly as possible. Now scan the face for details, observing the eyes, for instance. See each lash, the iris, and the fold of the eyelid. Next, focus on the lips. Continue observing the face for all the details. If any other thoughts come in, gently push them away and return to your visualizing.

If you find this exercise difficult to accomplish, ask that person to stand in front of you for a minute while you concentrate on his or her face. Then close your eyes and continue holding the image. The person in question can leave now. Record your results in the Workbook.

EXERCISE 3

Select a photograph of someone you do not know. A picture in the newspaper will work nicely. Concentrate on the picture steadily for about three minutes. Close your eyes and continue holding the image. If you lose the image, open your eyes and concentrate on the image for about ten seconds, then close your eyes again. Practice this every day for one week. Be sure to write down your results in the Workbook.

five

Symbols

Since the beginning of time, symbols have existed. The northern slopes of the Pyrenees are known for a concentration of Paleolithic caves, the best known being the Cave of Lascaux, in France. Here we would find prehistoric drawings of animals, people, and symbols.

Basically, a cave is a cavity inside the earth. Whether natural or artificial, caves have been important to the human species. They offer protection and shelter, yet can trap and imprison. Some cultures have identified caves as female, seeing them as the womb of Mother Earth, and some cultures consider caves to be sacred. During prehistoric times, the earliest known sacred places were naturally-formed caves, such as Lascaux. Caves were the place of mysteries, and many cultures used caves for celebrations. They were often the focus of religious stories and religious rites, because prior to the creation of temples, religious rites took place in caves.

Animals are depicted in great numbers on cave walls and appear to be much larger than other images. Horses are the most prevalent species depicted. Birds and fish are rarely seen, and humans are only shown once in the Cave of Lascaux.

In ancient times, people used symbols to communicate with each other. Today we would express our impressions outwardly, perhaps in writing or verbally, while in prehistoric times people scribbled in the dirt or on cave walls.

With clairvoyance, the use of symbols is a very common ability to acquire or experience. This is because everyone has had experiences where they have seen visually. Even someone who is blind from birth can have images of colors, shapes, and swirling masses. When we receive an impression during meditation or while going about our daily lives, a thought, a feeling, a picture, a sound, or a smell comes into the mind.

The mind has the ability to receive thought, but we don't register that thought unless we have two senses active. It takes two, as has been said before. When we receive a picture, we also have the power to interpret. In order to use the symbol (the picture), we have to utilize interpretation. How we interpret symbols depends on how we have lived, who we have known, and our life experiences, the same way we interpret other events in our lives.

It's our conditioning. For instance, a friend of mine has a teenage son who loves snakes. He has several snakes as pets, much to the chagrin of my friend. These two people would have opposite impressions if they saw a snake in a meditation. The son would see this snake as a friendly sign, a creature that brings joy. My friend, on the other hand, would see the snake as a scary creature, one that gives her no pleasure.

The use of symbols in this line of work is often helpful when it is necessary to have an emotional detachment. When we meditate for our personal enlightenment, it can be difficult to receive information about a situation because we are the ones involved. By using a symbol, we aren't emotionally connected to the issue. Therefore, the use of symbols is a wonderful means to employ when needing to create detachment.

The symbols that come into our minds and our thoughts spontaneously are specifically ours. While there are many books on symbols that define exactly what a meaning can be, the Rev. Diane Davis believes that symbols are actually unlimited. Therefore, she suggests that during a reading we exercise flexibility when interpreting how a symbol relates to an individual. Diane feels that the symbol is one of the purest forms of clairvoyance. For instance, if health is an issue, by using a symbol we are not becoming involved in the emotions possibly connected to the health issue. By *not* using a symbol, we would possibly project an inaccurate meaning onto something. Using a symbol can help to eliminate this conclusion.

By deliberately choosing to use a symbol, we can effectively take ourselves out of our personal lives and thoughts, and focus on something neutral. After all, all of us experience stress in our lives. When giving a reading or seeking an impression to answer a concern, we need to be detached and unemotional. If we are under stress due to our mother being ill in a nursing home, for example, we can clear away our personal mind chatter by focusing on a symbol.

Some professionals work entirely by utilizing symbols, defining and interpreting one symbol, then proceeding to the next, and so forth. Symbols also provide a picture for the person we are reading. Some people do not enjoy working with symbols because they simply do not like them, do not feel comfortable with them, or they did not learn to effectively work with symbols when they were training. It is a very personal preference.

For people who are reluctant to use symbols, their biggest concern is that they will not interpret the symbol correctly. However, there is no right or wrong interpretation because the interpretation should be based on how we feel about the symbol due to our life experiences. That's when that second sense I spoke about earlier assists with the interpretation.

We also have literal and symbolic meanings to consider when working with symbols, which certainly could confuse the issue of interpretation for someone who dislikes using them. Let's take the symbol of a baby, which happens to be a common symbol. The symbol of a baby usually means a literal translation of a birth of an infant, but it can also mean the birth of a new endeavor, such as a business or a creative project. We must also recognize that our interpretations of specific symbols can change over time. As we grow and mature in our spiritual evolution, our interpretations may take on different meanings.

Frequently, when an article comes into our mind, it is being delivered by a spirit entity. The spirit is using an object as an identifying mechanism so a person will recognize the spirit that is trying to communicate. Let's use the image of a gold, heart-shaped locket. This locket may have belonged to a great aunt and now is in the possession of the person receiving the reading. However, it could also be that the locket is being given symbolically to the client as a gesture of love. If this is the case, we are asked to interpret the meaning of that locket in relationship to this person instead of the obvious literal definition. With practice, we learn through using other abilities, such as clairsentience, whether we should interpret literally or symbolically.

Let's consider what the gold locket image is showing us: gold is expensive; the locket is heart shaped; it's hanging on a very long chain, but the chain is tarnished. We could interpret this to mean that all is not as it appears to be in affairs of the heart. This could mean that a long-term relationship is becoming less fulfilling than it was in the beginning. Now, if the locket had appeared to be bright gold, dangling on a normal-sized chain, we could interpret this to mean that a new love has entered the woman's life. Then again, maybe you would have another interpretation based on your experiences in life.

Warren does not personally interpret the symbols he receives—the interpretation is automatically presented to him. The spirit just tells him the interpretation. Sometimes there is what he calls a "keystone symbol" in a scene that the whole message is built around, sort of like when we see a keystone in a brick arch. Warren says that when this occurs he builds on the keystone for the interpretation and that way he automatically picks up on the interpretation. Sometimes sound, another gift, also contributes to the interpretation for Warren.

We interact with symbols on a daily basis. A traffic light, for instance, is a symbol. So is a school, a church, a house, a car, and a ring. Symbols are all around us. Since we are surrounded by them, we need to practice working with them in order to express our individual interpretation of the symbol. Like anything else with the development of clairvoyance, it takes practice, trial, and error.

It may be worthwhile to purchase some dream interpretation books to provide you with a generic definition of symbols. However, if you see a symbol during meditation and the interpretation of that symbol shown in the book doesn't feel correct, you don't have to accept it. First and foremost, what does the symbol mean to you? What was your first impression? How did the symbol make you feel? How does the symbol relate to your daily life? What negative or positive associations are present with the symbol? The answer to those questions is the correct interpretation.

The following cannot be emphasized enough: Interpretation is highly individual. The obvious is not always true. For instance, when we lead students in a meditation exercise, we usually say, "Go to your favorite place in nature." That works just great for most people, but not all. I once had a student who was raised in the city. This was a girl who thought that if you ate on a picnic table, you were camping out and roughing it. Going to a place in nature was not a relaxing experience for her, which was the opposite intention of the meditation. Her interpretation of nature was that it was a scary place, full of bugs and danger. Therefore, her interpretation of the great outdoors would not be the same as a person who enjoys fishing on the weekend.

Arlene sees symbols as being a cooperative effort between the spirit and herself so that the spirits don't have to pound the message into her head. For instance, when she sees a yo-yo while tuning into a person's finances, Arlene interprets that to mean an up and down, yo-yoing financial situation in the client's life. For Arlene, symbols are a clear indicator of accuracy, and she receives certain ones, like the yo-yo, regularly.

Phoebe believes that we each have our own set of symbols due to the experiences we have had in our lives. Let's consider that Phoebe was raised as a Catholic. As such, she remembers having a Saint Christopher medal hanging on her rear-view mirror for protection of her car. If Phoebe sees this item now, then it is a signal for her to convey protection to someone else. When Phoebe saw a Saint Christopher medal associated with a woman, she felt it was a sign that the woman needed to be careful because there was a need for protection. This was an excellent way for a spirit to convey that message of protection.

Sometimes during a reading I will see a generic nun. When I ask the client if he or she has a Catholic background, the answer is invariably "yes." Although I have never been Catholic, I associate nuns with Catholicism, so the spirits give me this symbol to identify the client as Catholic.

You will enjoy how spirits present symbols to you. Be open to the various interpretations you will receive. Also, you can deliberately select a symbol to use when answering a question. A tree is an excellent symbol to work with because you can easily apply trees to a particular situation or question and then interpret what you see. For instance, a tree can have a full, leafy top or no leaves at all; heavy limbs or thin branches; a thick trunk or a flexible, long trunk; and roots exposed or buried in the ground. With a tree, there is a lot to use for interpretation.

As an example, let's say that in our meditation we ask for a tree to symbolize a relationship. The tree we are given has a lush, full top to it, and it is big and bold in its continence, with two severed branches. If we had seen broken branches, that would have suggested broken relationships or divorces. But our tree has three places where branches have been severed, giving us the possible meaning that people who have passed away were of primary importance in this person's life.

If we ask for a tree to symbolize a health issue, the tree we see may have a healthy looking trunk, but one side may appear a little lighter in color. Perhaps this could mean that there is difficulty in the intestines or abdomen.

To find out how a person is progressing in his or her life, we look at the location of the roots. For instance, if the roots are suspended above the ground, this could mean that he or she is not well grounded at this time. This could be an emotional condition rather than an example of how conditions in life appear on the outside.

Other considerations are: Is the tree sturdy? Is it fragile? A weeping willow would mean something different than an oak tree. A weeping willow may be associated with fond childhood memories. A flowering tree, such as a dogwood or azalea, would give another impression. Perhaps flowering trees make your allergies flare. That could be interpreted as a warning.

Now that you have these examples, you can see how important it is to understand how the symbols relate to you personally and how to identify them in relationship to a person for whom you are attempting to read or a situation you need to understand within your own personal life. If you are stumped for a definition or interpretation, simply ask to be given the answer.

Exercises

EXERCISE 1

Next to each word, write about what the item means to you personally.

Ring:

Flower:

Cat:

Dog:

Snake:

Bird:

Fish:

Tiger:

House:

Car:

Baby:

Stuffed Animal:

Cup:

Knife:

Rifle:

Hand Gun:

Book:

Shoe:

Pencil/pen:

Hat:

Glasses:

Bed:

Chair:

Table:

Plate:

Stairs:

Door:

Window:

Angel:

Music:

Piano:

Guitar:

Hamburger:

Water:

Ball:

EXERCISE 2

Using your symbol of choice, ask that the symbol be shown to you in reference to a current situation in your life. Write down your conclusions in the Workbook (page 145). You may find that the symbol you chose will change after you have worked with it for a while.

Exercise 3

Ask to be shown a symbol in association with a person. Be careful not to take things you see too literally. For instance, a big tree means a strong tree, usually. So let's say that you see a large tree. Your interpretation could be that this is a strong person, maybe. Look deeper. How is the bark appearing? Where is the tree located? Is this a northern tree situated in the desert? Maybe this person is not feeling at home and not surviving well where he or she is located presently, and is experiencing difficulty. In other words, expand on what you see. This takes practice, so don't be discouraged if this exercise doesn't come easily. Write down your determination in the Workbook.

Exercise 4

Using your personal symbol, or asking to be given one to interpret, inquire about the outcome of a future event. Interpret what you see carefully according to your feelings about what you see. Be sure to write down the results in the Workbook.

six

Other Forms
of Clairvoyance

Besides the standard ways we can anticipate experiencing clairvoyance, we may be fortunate enough to develop some less commonly experienced forms. This chapter will touch on x-ray clairvoyance, medical clairvoyance, traveling clairvoyance, and visions.

X-Ray Clairvoyance

X-ray clairvoyance is a talent that we do not often hear about. As the name suggests, x-ray clairvoyance is the ability to see through physical matter. For example, let's suppose a watch is placed inside a box. Having no prior knowledge of the content, a person with this unique ability would be able to see the watch inside the box.

Another example would be a handwritten letter that is sealed inside an envelope. A person with x-ray clairvoyance, having absolutely no knowledge of the subject of the letter prior to the exercise, would be able to read the letter, possibly line for line. There are even instances recorded of clairvoyants reading sealed letters in unfamiliar languages.

Medical Clairvoyance

Medical clairvoyance, another less common ability, was first acknowledged by Hippocrates, and then, in 1831, the French Academy of Medicine also recognized medical clairvoyance. Andrew Jackson Davis, known as the Poughkeepsie Seer (1826–1910), was credited with this ability. Although basically illiterate and uneducated, Davis, while under a trance state, was able to accurately diagnose disease in the human body.

Education has absolutely nothing to do with clairvoyant abilities. In America and England, there are records of uneducated servant girls who, while working for doctors, were able to demonstrate this phenomenon. One example took place in Wrentham, Massachusetts, in 1844. While in a trance state, Mary Jane, the servant of Dr. Larkin, was able to diagnose, with remarkable accuracy, illnesses within the doctor's patients, as well as her own ailments. In England, around 1849, Emma, the handmaiden to Dr. Haddock, described a heart as she saw it in terms she understood. She called the auricles, the ears, and the ventricles "meaty parts."

A medium with whom I once had an acquaintance had the ability to diagnose illnesses through medical clairvoyance. She worked with a surgeon in a college town where there were many doctors. She would travel to the surgeon's office once a week to work with him. One time she was called upon to ascertain the nature of an ailment that another physician had been unable to determine, which resulted in the patient having surgery. Once the surgeon performed the operation, he was able to evaluate the accuracy of her diagnosis. Additionally, having prior knowledge of what to anticipate, the surgeon was more prepared for the surgery.

The famous psychic Edgar Cayce was well known for his ability to diagnose illnesses in people who were at a distance. While in a hypnotic state, Cayce would ascertain the difficulty being suffered and even suggest the cure after receiving only the name and location of the individual. Many books have been written about Edgar Cayce and are readily available if you want to explore this field further.

Arlene used to have medical clairvoyance. For the first five or six years during her formative years of spiritual development, she was able to see a person's body without clothes or skin, as if she were looking at an x-ray. Arlene saw the bones and systems, and would see a magnified area that was indicative of where the healing was needed. To her regret, she does not possess the ability now.

One evening during class, Carol decided to give her students an exercise on medical clairvoyance. She had one of the female students stand against the wall so the rest of the class could practice their x-ray vision. Carol was the only one who was aware of the woman's ailments, since the woman had previously been to Carol for consultations. Carol directed the members of the class to psychically go into the body and then move down the body. During the scanning expedition, she directed them to stop at areas of the woman's body that they felt were affected. Remarkably, all the students accurately read where the problems were in the woman's body.

Silva Mind Control, a course originated by Jose Silva, is another method in which practitioners are taught to enter a body psychically in order to read the ailments and disorders of an individual. Students are also taught how to remedy the situation with the assistance of their "counselors." This is a fascinating course, and one I highly recommend for anyone who wishes to generally develop his or her psychic abilities.

Traveling Clairvoyance and Visions

Traveling clairvoyance dates back to primitive people, when shamans and medicine men were the ones who frequently demonstrated this ability. When we consider that Andrew Jackson Davis received no formal education yet was able to perform as a medical clairvoyant, it is easy to speculate that we could master, at the very least, traveling clairvoyance. Traveling clairvoyance is a talent that can be totally natural to possess and may occur either purposefully or spontaneously. Today's terminology would use the phrase "remote viewing" to describe this ability.

There are many recorded examples of traveling clairvoyance, dating back to the 1700s, where a person under hypnosis could describe actions taking place at a distance. In 1785, a young girl in a hypnotic state described the actions of the person who put her into hypnosis after he had gone into town to conduct his business. She was able to describe everything happening around him in the town, as well as what he did while he was there. There are records in various countries of similar circumstances that support this unique claim.

The following is an example of spontaneous traveling clairvoyance: In 1756, while in Gothenburg, the Swedish seer Emanuel Swedenborg (1688–1772) had a vision of a fire in Stockholm. This event was witnessed by many and was later written about in 1758.

Maude Kline was a well-known medium in Camp Chesterfield in the 1950s. Although she did materialization and direct voice séances, her specialty was traveling clairvoyance. To perform this feat, all Maude needed was a person's name and address. She would psychically travel to the person's house, describe what it looked like outside and inside, and even discuss the contents inside.

Whether under hypnosis or experiencing spontaneous traveling clairvoyance, it is an ability that could be useful to some and, at the very least, it is an enjoyable exercise. However, I would caution you to use integrity. Once, while living in an apartment in Winter Park, Florida, I was talking to a girlfriend on the telephone. I was wearing a nightgown and sitting on the couch in a fashion reserved for my private moments. Suddenly, I became aware that I was being watched, although I was alone in the apartment. It felt like someone was standing in front of me, observing my actions. And, to make matters worse, I knew who it was! Feeling exposed, I quickly assumed a more discreet position on the couch. Later, I asked a particular psychic I knew who lived thirty miles away from me if he had been visiting me in my apartment at that particular time. He admitted his visitation and accurately described what I was doing. Naturally, I felt my privacy had been invaded, so I told him not to pay me any more visits like that again! That is a clear invasion of privacy, and it is definitely an unethical practice.

Many people are very interested in learning how to do remote viewing. Carol taught a class in Milwaukee about remote viewing and was amazed at how well the entire class did. First, Carol selected three target destinations. She then had the students either write or draw what they saw. Considering that they were ingénues in this talent, they did remarkably well, giving such details as colors, shapes, and descriptions of objects.

It would be easy to confuse a vision with traveling clair-voyance. Traveling clairvoyance is either a deliberate action or a spontaneous occurrence. A vision is spontaneous, something we cannot will to happen. Additionally, Rev. Jim Watson feels that another difference between traveling clairvoyance and the experience of having a vision is that in a vision we are on the sidelines observing the sequence of events without feeling any emotional attachment. However, in Jim's experience, when traveling clairvoyance occurs the emotions are very much involved. Also, visions can be pre-cognitive—a viewing of something that will happen, but is not currently occurring. Most of Jim's experiences have been spontaneous traveling episodes rather than purpose-ful acts.

During the traveling clairvoyant episode he had in 1974, Jim felt emotional involvement. This episode began when Jim was resting in a recliner. He was thinking about his plans to travel to northern Florida for the weekend to fish with his brother. There was a special bond with this partic-ular sibling because the brother was born shortly after Jim's birth. While Jim was in this relaxed state on the recliner, he began to see a scenario play out in front of him, much like watching a movie or a television show. Jim saw his brother being pulled through the wench on a fishing boat. This was a highly unpleasant scene to watch, and, consequently, Jim reacted emotionally. He wanted to do something to stop what was happening, but he was helpless. Jim's father called

shortly thereafter to tell Jim that his brother had died trag-
ically. The accident happened exactly the way Jim had seen
it unfold, and it happened at the same time that Jim had
the vision. Jim's brother was only eighteen years old when
he passed.

Visions can enable some to receive a signal of upcoming
events. Robert James Lee had visions of the crimes Jack the
Ripper was going to commit the day before the murderous
events. He even gave exact descriptions of the area where
the murders would occur.

Warren concurs that there are times when we just know
that what we see through traveling clairvoyance or visions
cannot be changed. Then there are what he calls "omen premonitions." This is where we see an accident, but we realize
that it doesn't have to happen. In a situation where an accident doesn't have to occur, there are no karmic ties, and
therefore we are allowed to change the outcome. But if there
are karmic ties present, the situation cannot be changed because it would affect other people. Warren feels that the
scene will tell us if what we are seeing is an omen premoni-
tion or not.

As an example, let's consider that there is the possibility
that a person might trip and fall. The scene might show us
steps, which could be a warning that the person should
take special care around steps for the next couple of weeks.
Sometimes the scene might be detailed enough to show a
specific location where an accident could happen, like at

the mall or in the home. Warren feels that by relaying the scene to a client, the spirit is placing the responsibility on the client to avoid an incident because he or she has been warned. Then it is the client's fault if he or she doesn't heed the warning, not the fault of the spirit world or the medium.

During meditation it isn't unusual for spontaneous visions to pop into our heads. Actually, this is the appropriate time for a vision to occur since we are in a wide open, receptive state. Once, while Phoebe was giving a telephone reading to a woman, Phoebe experienced a vision. She asked the woman to whom she was giving the reading if she knew anyone who worked at NASA? The woman responded, "No." Phoebe asked her again, "Are you sure? There's something here about NASA. I saw the space shuttle, and then it disappeared." The woman still did not identify with that. However, two weeks later the space shuttle exploded.

It is unknown why this information came through that particular woman to Phoebe, especially since the woman had absolutely no connection with NASA or space. Phoebe was simply open to receive that message from the Universe. Frequently, there are never any explanations given for why we receive spontaneous visions of future occurrences.

Arlene had a profound vision during a séance with the world famous healer Dr. Olga Worral and her husband Ambrose, both now deceased. The séance was conducted at the Worral's church in Springfield, Massachusetts. Arlene said the vision she experienced was crystal clear and intense. It wasn't a "snapshot quickie," but a pronounced power saying this was going to happen, no matter what. Arlene's vision revealed a bunch of coffins in a sports arena where all the flags were at half-mast. Arlene knew this was an event that could not be prevented by her or anyone else. Because this realization came from a place of knowingness that was so intense, she knew it was real and inevitable. This was in 1972, right before the assassinations at the Olympics.

Occasionally, Phoebe will receive flashes, similar to the NASA incident, where she gets information that is unrelated to the reading she is doing. Phoebe feels she must be touching into another time frame or spiritual plane when this occurs. This ability started when Phoebe was in her midthirties and would experience visions while in a dream state. However, Phoebe felt very uncomfortable about these visions because they were scary dreams! Once, Phoebe saw a busload of kids go down over a mountain cliff. Another time she saw an airplane crash. A week or two after the flashes, she read about the events in the newspapers.

Because Phoebe was upset by these visions, she eventually called her mother to tell her about the prophetic dreams. She told her mother that she didn't want these kinds of dreams and she didn't want to know about these coming events. Her mother told Phoebe that for the next couple of nights before she went to sleep she should state that she did not want *that kind of dream*. Phoebe followed her mother's instructions, but she neglected to say "that kind of dream." Instead, she stated, "I don't want to *dream*." Consequently, to this day, she rarely ever remembers any of her dreams.

One interesting thing that Phoebe experiences today happens at bedtime. Before falling asleep, she frequently sees spirit people in her room. Phoebe says it's as if a whole string of people from every nationality are passing through her bedroom. The spirit people look at her as they pass by, and then they keep walking. She often wonders, "Are these the ones who passed today?"

Spontaneous visions are not an ability one can work to develop. We either will have them or not. If you are fortunate to experience this phenomenon, be sure to record it in your journal.

Traveling Clairvoyance Exercise

After meditating to relax, ask your spirit teachers to take you to a particular destination. Choose a place where you will be able to verify your results, such as the residence of a college friend who lives in another state. I would suggest that you use a vehicle in which to travel when first attempting this exercise. The vehicle could be a cloud, a ball of white light, or wings, for instance. Visualize your vehicle of choice passing through time and space until it reaches its destination. Once there, observe carefully everything that you see. Items to pay particular attention to would be colors, objects, furniture, walls, and any people or animals present. If a person is present, what is he or she wearing? What color is the clothing? What is the person doing? Watching television? Speaking on the phone? Typing on the computer?

Please do not use this exercise as an excuse to invade someone's privacy. Choose a person who would be open to this exercise and select a time of day that would be appropriate, such as later in the afternoon when your friend is usually home studying or cooking dinner (and not a time of day when he or she could be in the shower).

Record your findings in the Workbook. Next, call the friend to verify your accuracy and note the results of the conversation in the Workbook.

seven

Psychometry

Working with psychometry is an excellent way to develop clairvoyance. The word "psychometry" means "to measure mind," and is derived from the Greek words *psyche*, meaning "soul," and *metron*, meaning "to measure." Psychometry is when we touch or handle something with our hands, and then receive an impression from the energy that emanates from the object or item.

Human beings are composed of energy, as is everything that lives. Trees, flowers, bugs, dogs, cats, cattle, bunnies, and green peppers all have life, therefore they all have energy. This energy is heat, and our bodies leave a residual behind after we leave a room or touch an object. This heat can be detected by infrared instruments. Detecting the information that remains from that energy is known as *psychometry*. We can sense and see information from the vibrations left on an object, or, in other words, we can "read" the object.

Diane Davis feels that everything in our existence is energy. Everywhere we've been, every word we've ever said, everything we've ever done, all the clothing we've ever worn, and everything we have ever touched has an essence of us absorbed into it. This is an excellent explanation of why we feel vibrations when we enter an old building. The residual energy from years back still remains inside the building. Another example would be entering a room that two people have just vacated after having had a verbal argument. That negative energy has been left behind. Those words are still present in the energy within that room, and we can feel it.

Psychometry isn't a parlor game to be used for the amusement of guests in our home, but it can be very helpful in our daily lives. To demonstrate the usefulness of psychometry, Diane ran her hand down a sheet of paper with a list of herbs printed on it, trying to ascertain which ones would be beneficial for her. When Diane felt heat, she stopped and selected that particular herb.

When we work with psychometry, sometimes an object feels like it is vibrating, or it is cold to the touch. This may simply be a means to get our attention, or perhaps the vibration or coldness is telling us something about the owner. Sometimes the sensation of cold or heat can be a way to get us to be aware of more impressions or thoughts. How we interpret what we see and sense will be based on our experiences in life, our education, where we've lived, who we've known, our backgrounds, our philosophy of living, and so forth. All the experiences we have lived through are stored in our knowledge. This is our personal database from which we draw to help us interpret.

When teaching students about psychometry, one common tool used in development circles is jewelry. Jewelry carries energy because it has been on our person. We have left a residual impression on the metal. But just as easily, a hairbrush could be used, a stuffed animal, car keys, or anything where a person has shared his or her energy. For this exercise, each person places an item of jewelry in a basket. Each student then selects a piece of jewelry to work with and, with eyes closed, holds the article in his or her hands and waits to receive a visual impression or a sense. Some people prefer to place an object up to their third eye or at their solar plexus, which is located near the belly button.

One misconception people have is that they sometimes assume that when they psychometrize an article such as a necklace, the necklace needs to be worn for a long time prior to it being psychometrized so that the energy is more intense. However, energy can be absorbed very quickly. To prove this during a workshop, Diane had the participants draw a little design with a colored marker on a wooden Popsicle stick. She told the class that drawing something as simple as two lines, or even writing their initials, was sufficient. The class did as they were in-structed, held the sticks in their hands, placed them into a basket, and then broke up into three groups. The individual students proceeded to read each other's Popsicle sticks with excellent results. This proved that wherever we go, whatever we say, we immediately place our energy there.

Another misconception is that there is only one energy present on an article. For instance, if you were given a ring that your grandmother wore while she was alive, it would carry her vibration, but if you placed the ring on your finger and began to wear it regularly, the ring would also absorb your energy. If someone were to attempt to read you through the ring, he or she would anticipate giving a reading about you. However, that person could also pick up on the energy being present on the ring of your grandmother. Therefore, it depends on the reader's intention when reading that particular ring. The reader should focus his or her intention on either you or your grandmother. With practice, the reader should be able to read all of the people who have worn the ring.

Psychometry has been used for many centuries in a conscious manner. We read about people touching an article and then having a vision or a flash of an impression. We also see this experience dramatized on television through movies. Animals, too, have the ability to sense when an object has been in another location and carries the previous energy in the new location. If this sensing brings a memory of a fearful experience, the animal will move away if it feels threatened.

Diane has found a variety of uses for psychometry to assist her when she needs to solve a problem. For instance, one New Year's Day while passing through Hollywood, California, Diane's car refused to start after a brief stop. All the car would do was churn, much to her chagrin. Obviously, this was not a good time to have a faulty-running vehicle. Diane psychometrized her car, received the answer she needed, and was able to continue on her journey.

In more recent years, Diane found that her car had been keyed on the side, with scratches running through the custom detailing. Again, she psychometrized her car. As a result, she felt that it was not specifically her vehicle that someone wanted to damage.

While psychometry can be playful and fun, it can also be a challenge. If we psychometrize an object when we are unaware of the ownership, it provides us with a neutral element to work with, similar to when we employ symbols. We aren't personally attached to the object so we can potentially receive from a point of neutrality. When we hold an object of unknown ownership, we are not caught up in someone's reaction, nor do we have any distractions.

In 1975, prior to her becoming a professional medium, Diane experienced an extreme example of psychometry. She had flown from Florida to Milwaukee, Wisconsin, to see someone she had known for a while. Another friend,

Jamie, was in Winnetca, Illinois, at the same time. A third friend, Sam, drove Diane to Winnetca to visit Jamie. The previous summer Diane had also made a side trip to Winnetca to visit Jamie. During the previous summer trip, the two women went to a play located on Clark Street in Evanston, Illinois, which will become important to remember later.

When Diane arrived to visit Jamie, Jamie told her that she was preparing to drive home to Florida in a few days, so Diane decided to ride with her. Before the two women departed for Florida, they decided to drive around the area. During the drive, Jamie got this crazy idea to find Sam, the friend who drove Diane to Winnetca. Both women knew Sam was in Evanston, Illinois, visiting his brother, but neither one of them had any idea where Sam's brother lived in Evanston. Since Diane thought she knew the brother's first name, the women drove into a gas station to look at a phone book.

The gas station was ready to close, and the two attendants working there appeared to be a little drunk, but were very sweet to the girls. Jamie asked one of the guys to look up the name of Sam's brother in the phone book and write down the address on a piece of paper, but not to show it to her. He did exactly as he was asked to do, probably thinking it was a sorority prank. Jamie did not look at what was written on the paper and returned to the car. She handed the paper to Diane. As soon as Diane touched the paper, she saw Sam lying down on a bed without a shirt on, facing the wall. The bedcover was plaid and the wall was green, with lots of bookshelves and books on the shelves.

Diane announced to her friend, "I'm going to take you on a wild goose chase, maybe." At this point Diane hadn't even looked at the paper, yet she began to give Jamie directions. She stated to Jamie that from what she was seeing, Sam was on the second floor of a building where there was a parking area and another building.

The girls found themselves at a stop sign on Clark Street, but not the same one from the summer before. Diane, not influenced by the previous summer, told Jamie to go around the corner. That's when they saw a high-rise, a parking lot, and another high-rise. One of the high-rises was smaller and located above a storefront. Diane pointed to the storefront building, indicating that it was that particular building they were looking for.

Diane and Jamie parked and entered the building. One of the names listed on the mailbox was Sam's brother. Diane started to shake. They pressed the buzzer and Sam's voice answered. Jamie said, "We found you!" Baffled about how the two women could be there, Sam told them to come on up to the second floor.

When Sam opened the door, he was not wearing a shirt because he had been lying down. Diane and Jamie looked across the room and saw a plaid cover draped over a daybed. The walls were green and there were lots of book-shelves from the floor to the ceiling. At this point, Diane had to sit down.

This journey of discovery took forty-five minutes. At no time did Diane look at the piece of paper with the address written on it, nor did Jamie. Amazingly, Jamie never had the urge to go to the other Clark Street while search-ing for Sam. This is truly a remarkable example of psy-chometry.

When I am traveling, I enjoy visiting historic buildings. I remember one fall when my husband and I were doing a driving tour up the east coast. We explored such places as Williamsburg, Virginia, and Washington, D.C. Oh, the fun I had psychometrizing the old homes! Savannah, Georgia, also provided an extremely interesting psychometry exer-cise. When we were in Savannah, the movie *Midnight in the Garden of Good and Evil* was very popular, so we took a tour, which was a fabulous means for getting impres-sions of happenings that occurred many decades ago. Of course, the tour included a cemetery, which was really powerful.

When I was on a vacation in Mexico, I was eager to visit the ruins at Chichén Itzá. I was sure there would be vivid impressions to receive from that ancient environment. I was not disappointed. When I placed my hands on the walls of the ruins, I received impressions of virgins being sacrificed or used in a ceremonial manner in association with that area.

While Diane was visiting California, as a favor to a friend, she placed her hand on an artifact, except it wasn't actually the genuine artifact, but rather a poster of an image of a place. So, basically, Diane was psychometrizing the name of the place. When she started talking about this locale, she felt a hallucinating energy. This hallucinating sensation was an indication to Diane that she needed to open her eyes to something. She knew she needed to pay attention to what she was allowing her energy to move and combine with.

In this particular situation, when Diane was focusing on the place, she realized that some people at this location were using hallucinogenic drugs during their ceremonies. If we encounter a mind-altering sensation while psychometrizing, it is important to remember not to allow our senses to move and combine with the drug. We must be able to detach from that energy so we don't feel like we are hallucinating. Once we recognize the situation for what it is, we can detach. Therefore, remain alert to outside influences.

Diane advises us that when we find ourselves sensitive to something like this, we should see this as a sign to open our eyes to what we are focusing on. We need to see something more clearly; all is not as it appears to be.

EXERCISE 1

Gather six to eight identically sized and colored envelopes. Sprinkle a spice inside each one. Choose salt, pepper, mustard, basil, sugar, cayenne, and so on. Mix the envelopes up so you cannot distinguish one from another. Practice sensing which spice is inside each envelope. Handle the envelopes until you are able to identify the contents of any of the envelopes simply by psychometrizing them.

Record your results in the Workbook (page 145).

Exercise 2

During your next vacation, be sure to visit historical buildings and old churches. Pay close attention to the impressions you receive while in the buildings. When possible, touch the side of a wall. What do you feel? Warmth or coolness? Is there agitation in the room or a peaceful feeling? What do you see? Do significant objects come into your view? Are there faces of people? Animals? Are there any odors present when you touch the walls? What is your interpretation from what you are seeing and sensing?

Write down your impressions, and when you return home, record your results in the Workbook.

Exercise 3

If your car, washing machine, VCR, or refrigerator should go kablooey one day, psychometrize it to figure out what's wrong. Can you see parts that are affected? Is there a noise associated with the impressions you are receiving? Do symbols present themselves as a means to convey the message?

Ask how this situation can be remedied? Who should you call for help? Should this be a friend or a business? What is a reasonable amount of money to expect to pay for a repair? Will the cure transpire today or will it take longer to accomplish?

Record your impressions and the final outcome in the Workbook.

EXERCISE 4

Get a take-out menu from a restaurant or use one you have stuck away in a drawer. Now, with closed eyes, run your fingers down the list of foods offered. See where your fingers are drawn. Notice the physical sensations you receive. Are your fingers cold? Hot? Do your fingers tingle from heavy spices? Does a sweet sensation pop into your mouth? What culinary images dance in your mind? Can you ascertain the name of the dish?

Write down all the images and impressions you receive, and then note your accuracy in the Workbook.

EXERCISE 5

The next time you receive a letter, psychometrize the letter before you read the contents. Do not open the envelope. What mood was the writer in when he or she wrote the letter? Does it feel like it contains good news or not so good news? Is there joy associated with the letter? Is there an announcement contained within? Is there a joke included? Are there recipes, newspaper articles, coupons, or ads inside the envelope?

Record what you experienced, and then note your accuracy in the Workbook.

Exercise 6

When selecting vitamins or herbs from your favorite store, hold the container between your hands. Do you feel that the product is right for you, or would something else be preferable?

When grocery shopping, touch the vegetables to decide which ones feel the freshest. Do the same for meat to see which is the best to purchase.

When a bill arrives, hold the envelope and decipher whether or not you will be pleased with the contents this month.

Run your hand over the television section in the newspaper to see where you are drawn.

While in the dressing room of a clothing store, hold the outfits individually in your hands and wait for an impression. What do you receive? "Too expensive." "I'll never wear this." "It will make me look fat, even if it is on sale."

For each item, write down your impressions in the Workbook.

Exercise 7

Have a friend bring an object to use for practice. Go into a relaxed state with soft music, taking some deep breaths, closing your eyes, and allowing yourself to melt into the chair. Methodically relax each part of your body until you are completely at ease. Have your friend hand the object to you. Hold the object comfortably between your hands, or place it next to your forehead or solar plexus, as some prefer. What do you see? Some possibilities include numbers, colors, words, faces, a location, a scene with people, and animals.

Once you have a visual, interpret what you see. How does it make you feel? Curious? Happy? Uncomfortable? Describe what you see to your friend, then give your friend your interpretation. If the object belongs to someone else, describe the personality of that person. Other impressions to look for in association to the owner would be his or her state of mind, health, character, past experiences, present situation, career, and so forth. The pictures that come into your mind will need to be interpreted. If the person appears sad, then say, "This is not a happy person."

Another approach would be to have your friend ask you questions. Sometimes the questions will act as a catalyst for you to receive impressions. Everyone works a little differently, so I would encourage you to experiment with other methods if one doesn't work for you.

Write down all of your impressions and the results in the Workbook.

To encourage the development of clairvoyance, use the techniques described in the previous exercises as often as you can.

eight

Practice, Practice, Practice!

This chapter is dedicated to furthering the clairvoyant development you have started or additionally enhancing your natural ability to be clairvoyant. It is recommended that you practice an exercise every day to enhance your abilities. How do we get to Carnegie Hall? You know the answer: practice, practice, practice! You should find the suggested exercises contained herein to be challenging and fun. As always, be sure to record your experiences and date the passage. Following this chapter is a Workbook, where I encourage you to enter any pertinent comments, such as, "This method works better for me than the previous one," or, "Several days later I actually did see the pink puppy: George gave me a pink stuffed animal!"

EXERCISE 1

This exercise can be accomplished alone or with a partner. Use a normal deck of playing cards. If working alone, after becoming relaxed through meditation, shuffle the deck of cards. With the deck facing away from you, fan the cards out on a table or your altar. Select one card, but don't look at the face of it. Place the card between your two hands, close your eyes, and visualize a blank screen. Ask that you be shown the card's face. If you are not shown the face, ask to be shown the appropriate color. Obviously, it will be either black or red. Next, ask to be shown the suit. Finally, ask to be shown the number or title of the character. Turn the card over to check your accuracy. It is unlikely that you will be 100 percent accurate, so do not despair if the number or the suit is off. Select another card and repeat the process for a total of ten times to determine your percentage of accuracy.

Record the experience.

Exercise 2

With a partner working with you, have the other person hold up a playing card with the information side facing away from you. Determine which card it is by using the blank screen method. Visualize the screen, then ask to be shown the card. Tell your partner the card that you have been shown. Move on to the next card until you have accomplished ten exercises. Record your results.

EXERCISE 3

Allow yourself to enter into a relaxing meditation by using a guided meditation CD or tape. Visualize nothing in your inner vision. Ask that you be shown guidance for a particular circumstance in your life where you need assistance. Visualize a huge sheet of white paper that is rolled up and standing on one end. Watch as the white sheet of paper unfurls slowly open. When it has completely opened, observe what is depicted on the screen. Interpret what you see. If the meaning is not totally clear to you, ask that you be shown the meaning in terms that you cannot help but understand. Record your impressions for future reference.

Exercise 4

After meditating, visualize yourself going into a movie theater. See yourself sitting down in the very center of all the rows of seats. No one is in the room but you. A huge, white movie screen is in front of you. Ask to be shown something. Don't anticipate any particular item or scene, just remain open to receive whatever the Universe deems you need to know at this time. Whatever you see may have significance, or it may mean absolutely nothing to you. Often what we see in meditation does not have an obvious significant value at the time. What we are being shown may have to do with a future event or a situation that we are ignoring, and the message will become clear after a period of time has passed. This is why we record our impressions— so we can refer back to something that made no sense at the time, but now makes all the sense in the world. You must record everything, even things that appear to be really dumb. You just never know how significant it may become in the future. Later, when you reflect back on this notation, you will see relevance.

EXERCISE 5

Some mediumistic teachers teach the following particular technique: After relaxing yourself sufficiently through meditation, imagine a funnel, a telescope, or a long tube sitting in front of you on the floor. Pose a question you wish to have answered. Visualize yourself reaching to pick up the tubular object in front of you. Bring your seeing device up to one eye and look down the length of the tube. Let your eyes travel through the length of the funnel, telescope, or tube for several seconds, perhaps fifteen or thirty. What do you see at the end? What is your answer? Record your experience for future reference.

Exercise 6

The previous method can be used to receive a general message, or to give you guidance. After meditating, rather than posing a specific question, simply ask to be shown something that is relevant to the current conditions in your life. See yourself picking up the tubular object of your choice from the floor. Allow your eyes to travel down the tube to the end. What do you see? Is it a person, a scene, a symbol, or numbers? Interpret what you have seen and record the experience.

EXERCISE 7

Visualize a heavy, white velvet curtain in front of you. (You can also visualize a black curtain, if that is more conducive for you.) In the center of the curtain are two golden cords hanging loosely downward. Ask to be shown something of value to your spiritual guidance. Focus on the curtain for a minute or so. In your mind, prepare to see something. Now, quickly pull the curtain open at the center by pulling the golden cords apart. What scene do you see?

If you cannot determine the message at first, be sure to leave it in your notes. The true meaning will come to you. Allow yourself to be open to receive. The answer could come from the radio or be read in a newspaper.

As always, record your experience for future reference.

Exercise 8

Once you are capable of receiving messages clairvoyantly, attempt to control what you see. Ask for something in particular to be shown to you. For instance, ask for an answer to a question. Use one of the methods mentioned previously, such as a blank screen, and then ask the question. But keep it simple in the beginning by asking questions that can be answered with a simple yes or no response. For example: "Will it rain tomorrow?" "Should I get gas in the morning?" "Should I cook chicken for dinner?" You may see a yes or no answer appear in your mind. Then again, the answer could come in the form of a picture. A rainy scene or a chicken walking around a yard could appear.

As you become more accustomed to this method, your visual experience will intensify. For instance, if you were to ask about whether a coworker is really your friend, you would see a scene play out in front of you. The more advanced you are, the more detailed the scene will be. You may see the person in question discussing with another coworker your "peculiar" behavior, but the behavior being discussed has never occurred. This is a lie being perpetuated by your so-called friend. The meaning of this visual is quite obvious, and you have a clear answer to your question.

EXERCISE 9

Relax yourself sufficiently through meditation, then visualize a beautiful golden door. See it as very ornate and glowing. Ask that your spirit guide be shown to you at this time. Watch as the golden door opens ever so slowly. With each inch the door opens, let your anticipation grow. You are about to see one of your spiritual teachers! This is exciting. This is an entity that will work with you for many years to come and guide you in many endeavors. When the door is far enough open to reveal the spirit behind it, observe what the spirit looks like. Notice hair color, height, weight, and style of clothing. What is the gender? What other impression do you receive?

If your guide does not appear clearly enough to describe, keep trying each day until you are successful. Record your impressions for future reference.

EXERCISE 10

Get a book from your bookshelf. After meditating to relax, take the book in your hands and randomly open it. Place your right hand on the page without observing any of the contents. See what impressions you receive regarding the words written there, the thoughts being expressed on that page, or the content covered in previous pages. This is not an easy exercise and could take a lot of practice, depending upon your abilities. Be sure to record the experience.

EXERCISE 11

If you work in an office where someone takes phone messages for you when you are not available, this exercise will be of interest to you. When you receive a phone message, place your hand on the paper and try to determine why this person has called. Is the caller a man or woman? What business does he or she wish to transact? Is this a personal call? Who is the person calling? Does this involve a lunch date? Will you need to pick up bread on the way home or pick up a child from school? Record your results when you return home.

EXERCISE 12

Similar to the previous exercise, psychometrize your answering machine at home. Before playing back the messages, place your right hand on the answering machine. Write down your impressions. Can you name who called? Can you determine some of the reasons for the calls? Play back the messages and see how accurate you are. Record your results.

Exercise 13

Scrying is an old term used in psychical development. The purpose of scrying is to focus attention so we are not distracted. We learn to develop our inner vision by focalizing our psychical energies. Our monkey minds are so busy that it takes great concentration to be oblivious to distractions, but it can be done!

Select an object to focus on, such as a crystal, a shiny, metal surface, or a glass of water. Allow your eyes to go out of focus so that you are seeing with your "lazy eyes." At first you will probably observe a cloudiness or misty effect. Some people see stars, or you may see little lights or bright spots in the clouds. The light centers may, with time, open or expand. Faces or bits of scenery may be vaguely distinguished, but they will not be sharp images. Practice this method numerous times until you feel some success. Be sure to record your impressions.

EXERCISE 14

Warren truly believes in the effectiveness of the mirror meditation, claiming that it is almost foolproof. And it's so simple to do! Mirror meditation, sometimes referred to as mirror gazing, is similar to crystal ball gazing and is another form of scrying. Other items that have been used throughout history for this purpose are shiny metal, bowls of water or wine, and, of course, ponds.

It is necessary to be in a darkened room to perform this exercise. Select a chair that supports your body and neck that is comfortable, but not so comfy that you risk falling asleep. Place one lit candle behind your chair. If this doesn't seem to work effectively, experiment with the placement of the candle.

Sit in front of a fair-sized mirror, such as one you would find on a dresser. Your bathroom may have the perfect mirror on top of the counter space. Look into the mirror of your choosing with your "lazy eyes." In other words, don't intently stare into the mirror, but rather relax your gaze by allowing your vision to go out of focus. Forms and symbols may appear around you, or faces. However, the images seen aren't really in the mirror any more than if you were looking into a crystal ball. The images are in your head. The mirror is being employed as a focal point, similar to being in a darkened room where you can't see what's going on around you so your attention remains focused.

Record your results. Endeavor to practice this exercise at least several times a week, but preferably nightly. Eventually, you will have to pull away from this method because you can't use a mirror all the time, but this is an excellent method to employ to begin seeing clairvoyantly.

If you're interested in exploring this method further, Raymond Moody has a more elaborate approach in his book *Reunions: Visionary Encounters With Departed Loved Ones*. I would highly recommend this book to anyone who wishes to explore communicating with spirits in this manner.

Exercise 15

Engage a friend in a conversation. Ask your friend to describe something, such as going to a play, a work situation, or perhaps a funny incident with a pet. While he or she is talking, visualize what the person is describing—with your eyes open, of course. This should be an easy exercise. Record your results.

EXERCISE 16

While a friend is talking, focus your attention on something else and hold your attention there. You should fore-
warn the person of your intent so he or she isn't upset
when you have no clue what he or she just said. Your focal
point could be an image of a cat, a candle, a face, or anything else you may think of. While the person is talking,
continually focus on your chosen image. If the focus strays,
gently bring it back to the image. You will know you have
been successful if you truly have no idea what subject your
friend spoke about. This exercise could also be done while
on the telephone. Please record the results.

EXERCISE 17

Sit with a friend who is willing to help with this exercise. The perfect person would be someone who is also learning to see clairvoyantly. Have your friend visualize a number. Attempt to see the number with your eyes closed. Use whatever method that you have had the best results with in the other exercises (the movie screen, a funnel, and so on). Once you are able to see the number with your eyes closed, practice this exercise with your eyes open. The number should "appear" between you and your friend, or above the head or perhaps to the side of the person. Record your results.

Exercise 18

For this exercise it is important to receive permission from the other party with whom you are working. Ethics are important in this work, and it is not ethical to invade someone else's privacy. After relaxing yourself, take the other person's hand. The reason this is suggested is because you will receive the personal energy of this person through touch, or what is commonly referred to as "vibrations." This could be compared to psychometrizing the person. If you feel so moved, say a prayer. The following prayer is generic enough for most people:

Universal Mind, bless this encounter and bring to us the highest and best information possible. Thank you.

With your eyes open or closed, see what images come into your inner vision. Tell the other person what you see occurring currently around him or her, what issues are of concern, problems that are present at work, and so on, and interpret what you are seeing. Have the other party give you feedback to hopefully confirm the accuracy. Record your results.

EXERCISE 19

Sit with a trusted friend for this exercise. If it feels comfortable to do so, take the other person's hand. Say a prayer that is intended to invite spirit entities into this session. You may wish to use the following prayer:

Mother, Father, God, we ask that those from the spirit side of life who are relatives or friends come forward at this time to be recognized. We ask that they come with love and good wishes, and that they demonstrate the continuity of life through ways we can understand. And so it is.

This exercise is probably easier to be done at this stage of development with your eyes closed. After the prayer is said, wait patiently for any images to form within your inner vision. Anticipate seeing faces, hands, full-figured people, adults, children, the elderly, and pets. If the image begins as an elderly person, frequently he or she will become younger, or vice versa. This is merely the spirit's way of conveying an aging process by showing different stages of the person's life. It would be obvious to interpret that the person lived a long time if he or she appears elderly. The actions from a younger time that you see will be indicative of his or her past. Describe as fully as possible everything that you see: colors, flowers, style of clothing (this gives an indication of the date), hair color, jewelry, and any personality traits that become apparent from observation. For instance, if the person is skinny, waving his or her hands all around, and acting hyper, you could interpret that to mean an energetic, high-strung, or nervous person. All the images that come in should be described to your friend so that he or she can possibly identify the spirit.

Sometimes there will be a visit from a spirit that the person cannot identify. Tell the person to talk to a relative who would have known the person when the spirit was on the earthplane. Please record your results.

This is not an easy exercise. If you aren't successful the first time, don't be critical of yourself. Some people practice for years to see spirits, while others see with ease. This will happen at the perfect time for you.

Workbook

Afterword

If you have been practicing the exercises while reading this book, at this point you should be gaining confidence in your ability to see clairvoyantly. You are well on your way to either developing a new talent or an enhanced ability. Eventually, clairvoyance will become a reliable friend.

In order for clairvoyance to be a tool you can rely on for your decisions, big or mundane, it is important to continue the practice you have established. It's similar to playing the piano. In order to retain our nimble fingers, we must practice. Otherwise, we would plunk along on the keyboard, barely getting through the song, rather than doing the performance any justice. The same is true for developing clairvoyance. Without practice, you run the risk of becoming stale and your confidence level may decrease as a result. The exercises in this book can be used over and over again to help build your talent further. Keep up the practice.

Besides your practice sessions, life will present you with exercises. When I was going through my development process for mediumship, one of the other students in class said something that stayed with me over the years. She commented that she wished she could take classes every day so she would have more opportunity to practice. The implication was that the only time she could practice her skills was during class. Another student, who happened to be an attorney, looked at her and remarked that she could put what she was learning in class into practice every day of her life. He asked her if she came into contact with people at her job. "Of course I do," she replied. He further queried her, asking her if her life was perfect or if she was ever presented with situations to deal with. "Of course I have situations in my life that I have to deal with," she replied. "Well, then, you have ample opportunities for practice."

Look for daily opportunities to present themselves that will assist you in honing your skills to further levels. As they say about life, "It isn't reaching the goal that's important, it's the process."

Here's to you and your visionary eyes! May they always be sharp and accurate!

Namaste!

Resources
for Development

Cassadaga Spiritualist Camp
P.O. Box 319
Cassadaga FL 32706
386-228-3171 or 386-228-2880
www.cassadaga.org

Rev. Phoebe Rose Bergin, Rev. Jim Watson, Rev. Dr. Warren Hoover, Rev. Diane Davis, and Rev. Arlene Sikora
(Contact the Cassadaga Spiritualist Camp through the information above.)

Elizabeth Owens
www.elizabethowens.com and elizabeth@elizabethowens.com

Carol Roberts
Milwaukee WI
(Contact me [see above] for Carol's referral information.)

National Spiritualist Association of Churches
P.O. Box 217
Lily Dale NY 14752
716-595-2020
www.nsac.org
(You can find Spiritualist churches in your area through this website and connect to websites for Spiritualist camps, such as Lily Dale Assembly, Camp Etna, and Temple Heights.)

Lily Dale Assembly
5 Melrose Park
Lily Dale NY 14752
716-595-2442

Camp Etna
P.O. Box E
Etna ME 04434
207-269-2094

Temple Heights
P.O. Box 311
Lincolnville ME 04849
Camp Phone (June–September): 207-338-3029

Camp Chesterfield
PO. Box 132
Chesterfield IN 46017
765-378-0235
www.campchesterfield.net

Morris Pratt Institute
11811 Watertown Plank Rd.
Milwaukee WI 53226
414-774-2994
www.morrispratt.org

Silva International, Inc.
1407 Calle del Norte
P.O. Box 2249
Laredo TX 78044–2249
1-800-545-6463
www.silvamethod.com

Association for Research & Enlightenment
(Edgar Cayce Foundation)
215 67th Street
Virginia Beach VA 23451
1-800-333-4499
www.edgarcayce.org

Glossary

Alpha: The alpha brain wave is associated with inner levels of mental activity, tranquility, rest, and relaxation. It is also associated with inspiration, creativity, accelerated healing concentration, and ESP.

Astral Projection or Travel: An action where the spirit leaves the body during a sleep state or through a conscious effort and travels into a spiritual dimension or an area on the earthplane different from where the physical body is located.

Beings of Light: Spiritual beings that live in the hereafter, heaven, or spirit world.

Circle: To sit in circle is a phrase used to describe an action where people gather regularly, usually in someone's home, to meditate for the purpose of contacting spirits. There may or may not be a teacher present.

Development Class: This is where a person may learn to enhance his or her psychic and mediumistic abilities under the tutelage of an experienced teacher who is a psychic or medium.

Direct Voice: During a séance, a voice is heard that does not come from a person's larynx. The spirits materialize a larynx from a substance from the medium's body called *teleplasm*. Since the spirit voices are so faint, a trumpet made from aluminum is used to magnify the sound. The spirits levitate the trumpet and it is moved around the room.

Going to the Light: A phrase used to describe when a person ceases to live in the physical and his or her spirit is making the transition to the spirit side of life. When a person is dying and entering the spirit world, a brilliant white light is seen, according to people who have had near-death experiences. This phrase also has connotations of a higher spiritual presence, such as God.

Karma: This could be referred to as "lessons in life." Some religions and many people believe our souls come to the earth to work through specific issues, or karma, so that we may grow spiritually.

Manifest: The appearance of a spirit through numerous means, such as in a visible form, by sound, or touch.

Materialization: The appearance of spirit, whether objective or subjective, to the physical eye or subconscious mind, respectively.

Meditation: When one stills the mind and body through guided imagery, mantras, or soft music for the purpose of relaxation and/or gaining spiritual information from the spirit world.

Medium: A person who is sensitive to the vibrations from the spirit world. Mediums are able to communicate with those on the spirit side of life through various means, delivering information and assistance to those who ask. All mediums are also psychics.

Messages: Greetings, information, warnings, comfort, and advice that one might receive through the mediumship of an individual from a spirit. Usually these messages are brief and delivered to a group of people individually for the purpose of demonstrating the continuity of life. Spiritualists conduct Message Services as part of their religious services.

Mini Reading: An activity where a person sits for a reading with a medium for a short period of time, such as fifteen minutes, at a reduced fee. Many mediums will often offer this service to the public as a fundraiser for the church.

Other Side of Life or Other Side: The spirit world where one who has passed away goes.

Physical Phenomena: Used as a means to demonstrate the continuity of life. Some examples would be the materialization of a spirit from a cabinet, a trumpet rising, a table moving, or voices emanating from a person or object.

Psychic: A knowing, sensing ability. This ability is a mental act, such as knowing who is calling when the telephone rings or sensing that your children are in danger at a distance. Everyone is psychic to a certain degree. All professional psychics are not necessarily mediums.

Reader: Someone who gives mediumistic or psychic readings or counseling, often referred to as a medium or spiritual counselor.

Reading: An activity where a person visits a medium or psychic for the purpose of receiving information/assistance regarding his or her life. This term could also apply to someone who would offer tarot card services. Not all means of receiving a reading offer communication with spirits.

Séance: This term was popular in the 1880s and early 1900s when people would gather in a darkened room to contact spirits through various means. A more accurate and current definition would be when people sit in classes for development purposes. Technically, when one sits in a circle during classes, he or she is participating in a séance.

Spirit: This is a word that has several meanings. Spirit can be defined as a luminous, ethereal form, once human, that is now deceased and living in another plane of existence. It is also a term used for God or to denote a higher spiritual power.

Spirit Lights: Spirit energy from incarnate spirits who are making their presence known.

Spiritualism: A religion, science, and philosophy that believes in continuous life, based upon communication with those who live in the spirit world, as demonstrated through mediumship. Through such communication one is able to receive guidance in mundane and spiritual matters from spiritual beings who are knowledgeable. Spiritualism embraces personal responsibility, the golden rule, and the belief that the door to reformation is never closed.

Spiritualist: As the basis of his or her religion, one who believes in the continuity of life and personal responsibility, and endeavors to mold his or her character and conduct in accordance with the highest teaching derived from communion with the spirit world. A Spiritualist may or may not be a medium.

Symbol: Where an interpretation can be deciphered from seeing an object depicted during meditation or in a dream state.

Third Eye: One of the energy centers each person possesses; also referred to as a *chakra*. It is located between the eyes and slightly above the eyebrows. Sometimes referred to as the *all-seeing eye*.

Trumpet: An instrument used to demonstrate physical phenomena. It is usually made of light-weight aluminum, is cone shaped, and collapses into itself for storage.

Unfoldment: The hoped-for end result of sitting in circles or classes for the purpose of learning to communicate with the spirit world and eventually "unfold" their mediumistic abilities.

White Light: Representative of God or a higher spiritual power, filled with love and protection from all harm.

Bibliography

Brinkley, Dannion, with Paul Perry. *Saved by the Light.* New York: Villard Books, 1994.

Buckland, Raymond. *Buckland's Book of Spirit Communications.* St. Paul, MN: Llewellyn Publications, 2004.

Carrington, Hereward. *Your Psychic Powers.* Brooklyn, New York: Astrol Company, 1939.

Ellie Crystal's Metaphysical and Science Website. "Psychic and Spiritual Clairvoyance." Ellie Crystal, author/owner. http://www.crystalinks.com

Fodor, Nandor. *An Encyclopaedia of Psychic Science.* Secaucus, NJ: Citadel Press, 1966.

Gundlach, O. V. "Holland's Premier Psychic Artist Visits America," *Psychic Observer,* November 10, 1947, no. 220.

Leah, Frank, and Marcel Poncin. "Artists Who Paint the Dead," *Psychic Observer,* May 25, 1939, no. 17.

McLintock, James M. "Londoner's Diary," *Psychic Observer,* June 25, 1960, no. 519.

McVey, Frances Haines. "Automatic Painting," *Psychic Observer,* November 10, 1955, no. 412.

Moody, Raymond. *Reunions: Visionary Encounters with Departed Loved Ones.* New York: Ballantine Books, 1993.

Myers, Arthur. "Molly Fancher: A Remarkable Psychic Story," *Psychic Observer,* September 10, 1939, no. 24.

Owens, Elizabeth. *How to Communicate with Spirits.* St. Paul, MN: Llewellyn Publications, 2002.

Phenomonist. "Psychic Artistry Proof Not Only of Survival but Also of Communication," *Psychic Observer,* October 25, 1960, no. 527.

Pressing, Robert G. "Spirit Paintings by Precipitation," *Psychic Observer,* September 10, 1938, no. 2.

Psychic News Reporter. "Healer Draws His Guide," *Psychic News,* London June 19, 1965, no. 1724.

Riley Heagerty, N. "Spirit Portraits," *National Spiritualist Newsletters,* January to July Editions, 1997.

Smith, Fernando. "Young Artist Medium Paints to the Classics," *Psychic Observer,* June 25, 1958, no. 471.

Stratton, Fred. "Automatic Painting of Drowning Tragedy," *Light: Journal of Spiritualism and Psychical Research,* October 18, 1934, no. 54.

Wallis, E. W., and M. H. Wallis. *A Guide to Mediumship and Psychical Unfoldment.* Mokelumne Hill, CA: Health Research, 1968.

Recommended Reading

Bodine, Echo. *A Still Small Voice*. Novato, CA: New World Library, 2001.

———. *Echoes of the Soul*. Novato, CA: New World Library, 1999.

Breathnach, Sarah Ban. *Simple Abundance*. New York: Warner Books, 1995.

Buckland, Raymond. *Buckland's Book of Spirit Communication*. St. Paul, MN: Llewellyn Publications, 2004.

Cerminara, Gina. *Many Mansions: The Edgar Cayce Story on Reincarnation*. New York: Signet, 1978.

Dyer, Wayne W. *Manifest Your Destiny*. New York: Harper Collins, 1997.

Gawain, Shakti. *Creative Visualization*. Novato, CA: New World Library, 1978.

———. *Living In the Light*. Novato, CA: New World Library, 1998.

Owens, Elizabeth. *Discover Your Spiritual Life*. St. Paul, MN: Llewellyn Publications, 2004.

———. *How to Communicate with Spirits*. St. Paul, MN: Llewellyn Publications, 2001.

Shinn, Frances Scovel. *The Game of Life and How to Play it*. Marina del Rey, CA: DeVorss Publications, 1941.

Stearn, Jess. *The Sleeping Prophet*. New York: Bantam Books, 1967.

Walsh, Neale Donald. *Conversations with God*. New York: Putnam, 1996.

Williamson, Marianne. *A Return to Love*. New York: Harper/Perennial, 1992.

———. *Illuminata*. New York: Random House, 1994.